Through My Mother's Eyes
The Story of a Young Girl's Life as a Prisoner of War in the Santo Tomas Internment Camp

Michael McCoy
with Jean-Marie Heskett

 **Strategic Book Publishing**

Strategic Book Publishing
An imprint of Writers Literary & Publishing Services, Inc.
845 Third Avenue, 6th Floor – 6016
New York, NY 10022
www.strategicbookpublishing.com

ISBN: 978-1-60693-015-1

Printed in the United States of America

Book Design by Stacie Tingen

Mom
You are my enduring inspiration and strength.
All my love,

Michael

Author's Note

It was the summer of 1964 when I first heard the story of the doll. We were living on a small farm in Sonoma, California, and it was a beautiful, warm afternoon. My brother Tim and I were playing outside when we heard Mom call to us to come in the house. She told us that she had something that she wanted to share with us. I was eight years old at the time and my brother was seven. I am the eldest in a family of six children; there's me, my brother Tim, my sisters Shannon and Kathleen, and my two youngest brothers, Jack and Patrick. On this day, though, Mom wanted to speak to her two eldest children. She said she would speak to the others someday, too, when they were old enough to understand.

I recall that the room became quiet as Tim and I sat across the large dining room table and watched Mom open a wooden box. She removed a small doll from the box and placed it on the table before us. The doll looked very old; the colors in the dress were faded, and there seemed to be a dark stain of some sort on it. The face of the doll was hand-painted, and, although faded over time, you could still make out the delicate features of the eyes, nose, and mouth.

"Boys, this doll was given to me many years ago, when I was nine years old. I think both of you are old enough now to hear the story of this doll, and the story that led up to me receiving it." Mom poured us each a glass of cold milk, and the story began.

As the story unfolded, Tim and I were on the edge of our chairs with our mouths open, totally absorbed by what we were hearing. To this day I cannot recall how long we sat listening to Mom speak, but it was dark outside when she was through.

Today, I retell this story to you - a story based on the memories and recollections of my mother, Jean-Marie Heskett (nee Faggiano). It's a story that may shock and horrify you at times, but it also a story of tremendous love, courage, and hope.

Thanks for sitting at the dining room table with me.

Michael McCoy
Santa Rosa, California

Hope is the thing with feathers
That perches in the soul
And sings the tune without the words
And never stops at all
-- Emily Dickenson

In spite of everything I still believe that people are really good at heart.
-- Anne Frank, diary entry (Diary of a Young Girl, 1944)

Contents

Introduction

The year was 1945. WWII was in its final year, and the Americans had just liberated the civilian prisoners of war that were being held captive by the Imperial Japanese Army at the Santo Tomas Internment Camp in Manila, Philippines. On this particular day, an American soldier had shot and killed a Japanese guard in an exchange of gunfire near the camp perimeter. The American soldier approached the corpse and cautiously bent down and examined the body for souvenirs, knowing that certain items, like weapons and flags, were frequently booby-trapped. He searched for telltale wires, and, finding none, removed the dead soldier's *senninbari* "thousand stitch belt." A small doll, now stained with its owner's blood, fell from the loosened belt to the ground. It might've been a gift from the soldier's daughter. Who knew? The GI picked up the doll and stuck it in his jacket pocket.

The American soldier's name was Theo Tanner from Frederick, Oklahoma, a private first class in the First Cavalry. After the soldiers worked their way into the camp, Private Tanner saw a little girl who resembled Shirley Temple, but was much thinner than the child star back home. This little girl was one of the many American POW children in the camp. She was walking toward the main plaza when suddenly Private Tanner had an idea. He jogged a pace and caught up with the girl with the curly hair.

A reporter for "Stars and Stripes" magazine, Sergeant Sam Blumenfeld, was nearby and spotted the two in conversation. What he overheard and wrote down was printed in a later issue of the magazine under the headline, "A Smile in Burning Manila."

"Here little girl, this is for you."

"Oh, no, I couldn't take it. It's a Japanese doll."

"C'mon... it's a present."

The little girl looked at the doll in Private Tanner's outstretched hand.

"It does have a pretty face."

"Sure it does. Why don't you take it? A doll is a doll, no matter who makes it."

"Well, okay, but I'll ask my grandmother if I can keep it."

"That's fine," said Tanner. "Why don't you run along now and ask her?"

"Oh, I couldn't do that," the girl said. "She's in America!"

Tanner smiled and offered her the doll again. The little girl smiled back, and this time she reached over and took the doll from Private Tanner's hand.

At that exact moment, Sergeant Sam Blumenfeld moved his camera into position and snapped off a shot. It was a picture that he later considered one of the most special moments of his wartime experience. He never forgot the smile on that little girl's face.

Her name was Jean-Marie Faggiano. Many years later she would share a story with her children about her experience as a prisoner of war in Manila, and what led up to the day she received that doll from Private Tanner.

This is her story.

Chapter One

Manila, Philippines 1941

For Eugene and Eileen Faggiano, life was good. Eileen, my grandmother, was a popular member of the Manila Country Club set. Eugene, my grandfather, also known as Gene, held a top position with American President Lines, formerly Dollar Steamship Lines. They had two children, my uncle, James, and my mother, Jean-Marie. Eileen loved to dress at the height of fashion. Gene was a young and handsome man, his dark Italian good looks setting off her Irish ivory and rose. Their children, James (Jimmy) and Jean-Marie (also known as Jerry), were healthy, lively, and full of fun. The Faggiano family employed a fulltime cook, a lavandera (laundress), a chauffeur for their brand new Nash, an amah (female nurse) for their children, a gardener, and a houseboy. They had two pets, a large cockatoo named Hernando and an English springer spaniel named Corky. The latter was a gift from one of Gene's friends, a pilot from the Clark Field airbase to the north.

Eugene and Eileen loved the Philippines and were making long range plans to live there. Gene's job with the Dollar Steamship Lines took them to the Orient following the birth of Jimmy in January of 1934. They lived in Shanghai first, where their second child, Jean-Marie, was born on October 15, 1935. From Shanghai they moved to Hong Kong, then Cebu, and finally to Manila.

The Faggiano family lived in a beautiful and spacious house in Manila on Del Pilar Street. Their landlord was Aurelio Montinola, a wealthy businessman and son of a former senator. At the Del Pilar residence, upstairs from the Faggiano family, lived Aurelio with his wife, Juliana, and their seven children, Alice, Carmen, Teresita, Aurelio Jr., Roberto, Sergio, and Lourdes. Jean-Marie and Jimmy played nearly every day with three of the Montinola children, Alice, Lourdes (Lulu) and Teresita. The Montinola girls often brought their two dachshunds, Hansel and Gretel, out to play with Jean-Marie and Jimmy. The two families were very close. The Montinola family considered the Faggiano family more than just tenants; they considered them an extension of their own family.

During their stay in China, Jean-Marie and Jimmy were very close to their amahs and had learned much from them, including languages. Jean-Marie spoke fluent Cantonese almost before she had learned English. Jimmy's amah had been from the north, so he had learned mostly Mandarin from her. After two years in Manila, Jimmy and Jean-Marie could converse in a mixture of Vasayan, Tagalog, Cantonese, Pidgin English, and Spanish.

Anselma Lusardi was the children's amah in Manila; a gentle, easy-going woman who received her greatest joy in being with the Faggiano children. Jean-Marie loved the times when Anselma would read stories to them or take them to the movies or to the park across the street. And every night, Anselma would give the children a special treat: a Philippine dessert of boiled rice and tomatoes.

For Gene and Eileen, there were endless parties at the Manila Hotel, famous names and faces from the lofty circles of politics and business, movie and stage stars, dinners and dancing, Jai-Alai games. They felt that they had reached a level of success that they had only dreamed about before. Indeed, life was very good.

And then early one Sunday morning, on December 7, 1941, all of that would change.

That morning a Japanese carrier fleet launched a surprise air attack on Pearl Harbor with a raid that destroyed most of the American aircraft on the island and knocked the main American battle fleet out of action. The attack united American public opinion to demand vengeance, and the following day, December 8th, the United States and Britain declared war on Japan.

For Gene and Eileen Faggiano and their two children, Jimmy and Jean-Marie, their life was about to turn upside down.

Jean-Marie stood in the hallway and watched her mother and father as they hovered around the radio, listening to the news of the attack.

"I remember my father and mother looking at each other in disbelief. I was more worried by the look on their faces than I was of the news on the radio. My mother told my father that she didn't think there was any way that the Japanese would invade the Philippines. Dad didn't look so sure. He argued that if the Japanese had just blown up the whole Pacific fleet, then an invasion of the Philippines couldn't be far behind. He made a decision, though, for us to hold tight and wait it out. He was counting on the American forces and allies to come to the rescue quickly."

Because of the International Date Line, it was already December 8th in the Philippines when the attack on Pearl Harbor occurred. By that afternoon, the Pacific war had caught up with the Faggiano's. The first flights of Japanese bombers struck at just past noon. Clark Field, just to the north of the Faggiano home, was blasted repeatedly by countless waves of bomber attacks.

During the afternoon of the first day of the attacks, Gene got behind the wheel of his new Nash and drove, miraculously unscathed, all the way to Clark Field to offer his services. Over the years, Gene and Eileen had been friendly with many of the officers and pilots stationed at the base. By sunset, the Faggiano home was crammed full of wounded soldiers. Their beautiful rugs and expensive, spotless furniture were now covered in blood. On the same couch where Eileen had sipped tea with wealthy cosmetics industrialist Helena Rubinstein only a year before, medics were working frantically to keep injured young men alive.

"My mother gave Jimmy and me a needle and a pan full of alcohol. Our job was to help with the less seriously wounded men. We were joined by the Montinola girls, Alice, Lulu, and Teresita. Each of us spent the night pulling slivers of shrapnel from the flesh wounds of the men."

When Jean-Marie's pan was filled and heavy with shrapnel slivers and diluted blood, she would make her way out the door and would dump her pan over her mother's flower beds. She instinctively knew that the flower beds, her mother's delight only the day before, now counted for nothing.

"I remember that several priests, ministers, and rabbis came to the house and were spending most of their time with the more seriously wounded and dying men. Sometimes I would hear a priest giving a soldier his last rites, and my heart would sink."

As the medical corpsmen assumed more control of the situation, Gene stopped helping with the injured and took charge of the kitchen. More and more evacuees from the shattered airbase straggled into the house on their way to Bataan. Gene found himself cooking for over a hundred unexpected guests.

On the second day of the attacks, Clark Field was completely evacuated. The runway was useless, with deep craters across its length. Many American aircraft, caught by surprise on the ground, had been destroyed in the first hours of the fighting. The death toll was uncertain.

For two days, the Faggiano home was one of the field hospitals for the survivors of Clark and Iba Fields. Then, late on the afternoon of the second day, a convoy of army trucks arrived, and squads of medics hurried to load the wounded and the dead. Within an hour the trucks were heading out to join the massive retreat to Bataan. The Faggiano family was suddenly alone again.

"I walked back into the house with my family and, for the first time, it really sunk in just how much our house had changed. The front door was removed from its hinges and all the windows were gone. We had used the curtains as extra bandages. The lawn and flower beds were crushed flat by the boots of soldiers and the tread of truck tires. I looked out into the backyard and saw bloody field dressings hanging from the broken stems of my mother's roses. I went back inside and found our pet Cockatoo, Hernando, stiff and dead, lying below his perch. Dad looked at him and couldn't find any wounds, so we figured he probably died from nervous shock."

For a week, Japanese planes bombed and strafed Manila at will, still concentrating on the airfields and shipping ports, but dropping strings of bombs in non-strategic locations as well.

"We would be driving in our car and suddenly we'd hear the air raid sirens go off. If we were close enough, Dad would drive us to the nearby walled city of Intramuros and we'd take cover there. They had shelters for protection, and many of the local residents would go there, too."

Jean-Marie's neighborhood, bordering Clark Field to the south, was hit with increasing frequency. After a few near misses, Gene and Jack Cassidy -- Gene's close friend from the States and fellow co-worker at Dollar Steamship Lines -- began digging an air raid shelter along the side of the house. The shelter would be about five feet wide, fifteen feet long, and almost six feet deep. Gene planned to stock it with supplies, including canned food. Meanwhile, while the trench was being dug and the bombs came in too close, Eileen and Gene would put Jean-Marie and Jimmy behind a wall of mattresses in the most fortified room in the house, the bathroom. Incoming bombs would reveal their flight path by the sound they made as they passed overhead. Jimmy and Jean-Marie, after hours in the bathroom behind the mattresses, started becoming experts in predicting the moment when the bombs would explode.

"By the third day or so the bombing was really wearing on our nerves. You would hear the bombs walk across the land... first close, then farther away, then close again. Each time a bomb would threaten to fall nearby, my mind would go completely blank. In the air raid shelter, I'd grip the earth with both hands and brace myself with my feet. The earth would shake with each blast and my ears would ring and then go numb."

Four days after the departure of the medical convoy, Gene was surprised to see a solitary army truck pull up to the head of his driveway. A young boy in uniform, so young Gene could scarcely believe this kid could be in the army, jumped out of the cab of the truck and strode up to the front door.

"My father came out to greet the young man and asked what he could do for him. The soldier said that he was on a burial detail. The chaplain from his unit wanted him to check and see if there were any bodies left to collect from the makeshift home field hospitals before they moved on to Bataan. Dad offered him a Scotch, but the young man refused, saying that he didn't drink hard liquor. Dad then offered him a Coke, which he gladly accepted."

A few minutes later, Gene walked down the porch steps to join the boy soldier by the tailgate of his truck. Eileen, Jean-Marie, and Jimmy followed him out the door and sat down on the porch, curious about the first U.S. serviceman they'd seen for days. Gene noticed that the boy looked too young to shave.

"Dad looked over at the truck and asked the young soldier what he had in the back, then immediately wished he hadn't. Jimmy, Mom, and I didn't see what was in the truck, but the look on Dad's face said it all. The private threw open the tarpaulin flaps that stretched across the back of his truck. Inside were torn remains of human beings. All of the men were from Clark Field."

The driver pulled the tarpaulin shut, flashed Gene a cheery smile and jumped back in the cab of his rolling house of carnage. He thanked Gene for the Coke, and a moment later the sound of his truck was fading up Del Pilar Street.

For two weeks the Faggiano's, like most residents from the West, stayed inside their homes and kept out of sight. On December 22nd, over 43,000 Japanese troops hit the beaches of Luzon and began their massive invasion of the Philippines. The city of Manila was in chaos, and for an "enemy alien" to walk the streets was suicidal.

"One day, during the first week of the occupation, Dad was looking out the front window of our house and saw our British neighbor's eight year old son, 'Awful Albert,' standing by the street. We called him 'Awful Albert' because he had a habit of doing things that would not only get him in trouble, but everyone around him, too. Well, there he was, in broad daylight, carrying over his shoulder a brightly colored Union Jack flag. Suddenly, a Japanese troop carrier raced down the street and slowed up as it approached Albert. And what does Albert do? He proceeds to wave the British flag at the Japanese soldiers! My dad was petrified. He saw the Japanese driver turn his head in dumbfounded amazement. Miraculously, the troop carrier just sped up and moved down the street and out of sight. Dad went out to the street and, as he got closer to Albert, he could hear the boy singing to himself, 'Today I'm going to be an orphan... today I'm going to be an orphan!' We wondered what Albert's parents would do when they found out that their son almost brought the entire Japanese army over for afternoon tea."

Filipino friends and neighbors did the shopping for many of the families, and brought them news of events in the city and surrounding areas. The Faggiano family lived in a state of suspended animation, hibernating within the walls of their home on Del Pilar.

After the initial chaos of the invasion had settled down, the Japanese posted signs all over Manila announcing that all Spanish, Portuguese,

Swiss, and German nationals were free to move about the city, but all allied civilians were to turn themselves in to the Imperial authorities by January 14th. The Japanese further stated that anyone not surrendering by that day would be shot on sight.

"They told us to bring enough clothes for three days. Dad told us that we should leave most of our stuff at the house and just bring the clothes, like the poster said. He said that since we were civilians -- non-combatants -- that they wouldn't want to keep us. He figured we'd be free again before we knew it."

On the morning of their surrender, Gene got up at dawn, made a cup of coffee and walked in the garage. His new Nash had been a symbol of the successful lifestyle the Faggiano family had come to enjoy before the war began. Now, for the last two weeks, he had seen Japanese officers passing by their house riding in the back seat of captured American cars.

Gene finished his coffee, got in the Nash, and sat at the steering wheel. He turned on the ignition and listened to the engine for a few minutes. He really loved that car. It was the first new car he had ever owned. He sat a few extra minutes behind the wheel, and then cut the engine. Gene drew a breath, and then pushed hard on the key until it snapped off in the ignition. He then searched through his tools and found the same pickax that he and Jack Cassidy had used to dig the air raid shelter. He took the pickax and blasted out the windshield, the passenger window, and all four whitewall tires. He then opened the hood and, with about a dozen well placed shots, assured himself that the Japanese would never ride the streets of Manila in his property.

A large limousine pulled up to the main gate of Santo Tomas. The owner, Pedro, and his twin brother Ernesto, were national celebrities, champion Jai Alai players and close friends with Gene. Gene got out of the car and approached the Japanese sentry at the main gate. Gene had been coached by Ernesto, so when the guard glanced at him, Gene bowed low from the waist.

"Dad told the guard that we were there to surrender. The guard looked at my dad, then at the limousine, and then gestured with his bayonet for him to get back in the car. I saw Dad begin to argue, but the guard interrupted and said, 'No, you go.'

"Meanwhile, my mother was watching this whole scene from inside the car and decided that she could do a better job of explaining things. She opened her door and walked up to the guard and said, 'No, you don't understand, we are supposed to surrender today...'

'YOU GO!'

'No, we CAN'T GO! We *have* to surrender today... the posters say...'

"Well, the next thing you know the guard began yelling in Japanese and was marching towards Mom with his rifle leveled at her belly. Dad yelled, 'Eileen, get back in the goddamned car!' and suddenly we were driving away from the main gate of Santo Tomas."

As they drove away, bewilderment over the guard's refusal to allow them into Santo Tomas was suddenly replaced by fear. The posters all over Manila had clearly stated that anyone not surrendering by this day would be shot.

They tried again at a post office that had been designated as another check-in point for internees, and again they were told to leave. Pedro, walking back to the limousine, looked at Gene and shrugged. He lit a cigarette and leaned against the hood of his car. Suddenly, he began to laugh.

"Dad asked Pedro what he thought was so funny, and Pedro gestured with his thumb at one side of the hood and said, 'I forgot about these.' Sure enough, there were two small Spanish flags attached to the hood of the car, one on either side. Pedro said to Dad, 'I think I know why he wouldn't allow you in. He thought you were Spanish.'

"An hour later we returned to Santo Tomas University. Our second attempt to surrender was successful. The flags were gone from the hood and a new sentry was standing in the tiny guard box."

Jean-Marie Faggiano and her family entered the gates of Santo Tomas Internment Camp on the 14th of January, 1942.

She was only six years old.

Chapter Two

Internment

When the Faggiano's entered the gates of Santo Tomas Internment Camp in January of 1942, they, like the rest of the internees, were first given indoctrination on the rules of their stay. The rules allowed the internees some leeway with how they governed themselves, as long as they stayed within the rules. They were instructed that they would have to be responsible for their own welfare, which would include managing their water and food supplies, sanitation, education, and health care. All internees were to show the Japanese respect at all times, which included bowing. They were also warned about the severe consequences of noncompliance with the strictest rules, which included the ultimate unthinkable, trying to escape. All internees were then given a meal ticket and a building and room assignment. Women and young children were assigned to the Main Building and Annex, and men and young boys were assigned to the Gymnasium and Education Building.

Eileen and Jean-Marie were assigned to the second floor of the Main Building, and Eileen was designated as room monitor of Room 48. Their new living quarters would be cramped; Eileen and Jean-Marie found themselves among forty-five other women, girls, and children younger than six, inside a room designed for less than half that number. Their bedding consisted of a simple kapok mattress, a small pillow, and mosquito netting.

"We were all given meal tickets that allowed us our meals each day. Dad started getting concerned right off the bat when he looked at the meal ticket. He said, 'Didn't they tell us we only had to bring enough clothing for three days? Well, the meal ticket shows we have meals for the next *thirty* days. I don't think these guys know how to count!'

"We noticed that on each meal ticket, right below the words 'STO. TOMAS INTERNMENT CAMP MEAL TICKET, MANILA, P.I.' was another line. It read, 'Compliments of Pabst Blue Ribbon Beer.' Dad thought that was particularly funny, as it appeared that alcoholic beverages would certainly not be on the menu any time soon.

"Our meals were simple and consisted mainly of meat, rice, eggs, and milk. When regular milk was unavailable, we'd have coconut milk. Although the food wasn't bad, they kept the portions modest. There were just so many of us to feed, and the lines were always long. We received three meals a day and our meal ticket was punched for each meal we ate."

The new inhabitants of Santo Tomas found themselves in a swirl of mass confusion, as several thousand allied civilians struggled to make the university campus livable. Order quickly emerged out of chaos, however, and the first major step had been the election of an internee government to interface with the Japanese authorities. The next order of business had been the establishment of committees. Within a few weeks, several committees and sub-committees were formed, including committees for work assignments, children's education, internee recreation, construction, maintenance, entertainment, and religious services.

Most internees had work assignments, and Gene and Jack Cassidy worked together hauling food from the front gate to the bodega inside the camp. Food would be delivered to the front gate by the Red Cross and Filipino civilians, and Gene and Jack would load it in a large cart and haul it inside the camp. Sometimes Jack would push and Gene would pull, and on the next trip to the gate they'd switch roles. The two men developed a close camaraderie during this time. They were close friends from working together at Dollar Steamship Lines, but they never had to depend on each other like this before. Often times they would sing songs and tell jokes during the hauls. Sometimes, Gene would pocket a couple of camotes (Filipino sweet potatoes), and give them to Eileen, Jimmy, and Jean-Marie.

As room monitor of Room 48, Eileen had several responsibilities. She was not only accountable for making sure that all of the occupants of her room were present during roll call, but she was also responsible for the rationing of toilet paper. Paper was in short supply all through the camp, and toilet paper was no exception.

"Mom used to hand out five squares of toilet paper to everyone in the room, every morning. That was it. You had five squares, and if you lost them or needed more, well, you were out of luck, Chuck. There was a boy in our room who must've been about two years old or so, and the poor kid had a hare lip. Every morning he would end up perched on the toilet and would yell out to my mom, 'Auntie Aieeen, I need some more 'oilet 'aper!' It happened every morning without fail. This used to drive my mother nuts. One morning I saw her heading to his rescue with a couple of squares in her hand – probably from her own personal ration – and saying out loud, 'Someday, kiddo, I'm going to cram this toilet paper down your throat!' The room would erupt in laughter. That was my mother. What made it so funny was that most people in the room knew that this was a woman who, only months before, was used to mingling with the rich and famous and living the high life in Manila. Her idea of manual labor was ringing a bell for the servants. Now they were watching her running to a latrine with two squares of toilet paper in her hand for a squawking two year old. Although I dared not laugh in front of her, it was quite an amusing sight to see."

A children's school was started, and Jean-Marie was one of the first students in the newly formed first grade. Jean-Marie had two teachers named Rosa for her first and second grade classes, Rosa Harrah and Rosa Preiser, respectively. The classes were taught in a makeshift classroom in a setting that might've drawn the envy of a student back in the States; outside under spreading palm trees and without the traditional desks, paper, or homework. There were also extracurricular classes, and Jean-Marie took ballet lessons. She also learned a native Filipino dance called the "Tinikling," where she would hop in and out between two bamboo poles that were brought smashing together at ankle level in time with the beat.

Sports became popular with internees of all ages, including baseball, soccer, and gymnastics. Sports were a good diversion from the everyday realities of camp life, and were enjoyed by participants and nonparticipants alike.

"Dad loved all sports, but was especially fond of boxing. He had been trained as a boxer during his twenties, so he became a natural choice as manager for the young men of the camp. He held training sessions almost every day and organized a series of boxing matches, or 'smokers' as they were called, in a makeshift ring. My father even taught me how to box, which I think he ended up regretting later. Many times I'd want to play games that the boys played, and sometimes they'd laugh at me and tease me. I'd usually end up in a fight and, thanks to my father's boxing training, would end up giving them a 'run for their money' as Dad used to say. Of course, I usually ended up with a black eye of my own, and more than my share of scratches and bruises, but I started getting more respect from the boys. In fact, not only had I acquired a new reputation around the camp as a pugilist, but I also received a new nickname: 'Champ of the Camp!'"

The internees strived to create a feeling of community within the camp walls, and to this end they became involved in numerous camp activities. There was the "Secret Christmas Toy-Making Club," the men's "Barbed Wire Choir," the "Little Theatre Under the Stars," and the camp bazaar and swap meet. They established and started the publication of a camp newspaper, "Internews" (later to be called "Internitis"), and a humorous paper called the "S.T.I.C. Gazette."

As the population of internees grew, some of the men from the camp began building shanties, outdoor huts made from scrap wood and sheets of tin. These huts were built in the flat, open-spaced areas of the university. After it became clear that the internees would be staying for an extensive period of time, more sophisticated shanties were built. These shanties were made from native nipa palm leaves and bamboo, and quickly spread all over the campus. In little time, the internees began naming their new outdoor communities. There was Shantytown, Toonerville, Froggy Bottom, Glamourville, Jungletown, Jerktown, and Over Yonder.

"We even had streets, like Duck Egg Drive and Camote Avenue, which weren't really streets at all, but just narrow lanes between the huts. Names were given to all of these areas to provide a reference for location, since the shanty areas had expanded so much. The naming was also done to provide a sense of community. In a humorous way they sounded like our world outside the gates."

In the evenings before curfew, internees could enjoy formal dances and even movies -- harmless old Hollywood romances, preceding and ending with Japanese propaganda films. Dave Harvey MacTurk, who was generally known in the camp as Dave Harvey, was a good friend of Gene's. Dave was in charge of the Entertainment Committee. With the commandant's approval, Dave arranged to have music piped into the main plaza over loudspeakers from a phonograph player each evening after dinner and before curfew. Sometimes internees would sing songs that reminded them of home, like "Goodnight Sweetheart" and "Deep in the Heart of Texas." In the span of just a couple months, a small town society had come together from several thousand internees.

"My brother and I were amazed by all the things going on around us. This new life was unpredictable and strange, but it was exciting, too. I received good marks in school. I was enjoying learning new things, and I made a lot of friends with the other children in the camp. My best friend was a girl named Bonnie. We used to play hopscotch together almost every day. I was also close friends with another girl named Jean, and two sets of brothers; Bobby and Billy, and Pat and Jerry. Jimmy and I played with them every day."

During her first year of internment, Jean-Marie suffered from tonsillitis. One of the internees, a physician named Dr. Fletcher, made the case with the Japanese officers to let Jean-Marie go to St. Luke's, a local hospital outside of the camp, to have her tonsils removed. The officers agreed, and Jean-Marie was allowed to leave the camp with her mother and check into St. Luke's for surgery. A horse drawn carriage (caramata) was hired for their journey, and Jean-Marie and her mother were made to wear red arm bands to signify that they were internees.

"During the time I was at St. Luke's for my tonsillectomy, I made friends with several of the nurses and other kids on the same floor. The kids had a game to see how many flies you could kill in a minute. I must've been pretty quick, because I ended up swatting more than anyone else. I ended up getting a certificate for being 'Champion Fly Swatter' of St. Luke's. I thought that was the greatest thing.

"On the way back to the camp, Mom asked the driver of the caramata to stop by our house on Del Pilar. She said she only needed a minute. I had brought my teddy bear with me to the hospital, and Mom took the teddy bear inside the house with her. She opened the side of the bear, removed some stuffing, and sewed all of her precious jewelry and coins inside the legs, and a five pound gold bar inside the torso. When she handed the bear back to me she told me what she had done, and that I wasn't to mention it to anyone. The teddy bear weighed a ton! While inside, she also gathered up some extra clothes, some cigarettes and some candy, and hid those in a separate bag. Before returning to the camp we made one more stop at a shoe store, where Mom bought shoes for herself, Dad, Jimmy, and me."

The Japanese guards never checked their bags as they re-entered the gates of Santo Tomas. They also failed to notice the bulging teddy bear that the little girl with the blonde curls was holding in her arms. They collected the red arm bands and waved them through the gates.

The Faggiano's were Catholic, and there was a makeshift Catholic church inside the walls of the camp that they attended every Sunday. On December 8, 1942, Jean-Marie received her First Communion in the church from a Maryknoll priest from outside the camp. The Montinola family gave Jean-Marie a prayer book as a gift for this special occasion, and inside the front cover was written the following from three of Jean-Marie's closest friends and playmates from her days on Del Pilar:

To Little Jean-Marie, A little remembrance of your First Communion. Lulu, Teresita and Alice

"Every time I'd read my prayer book, I'd think of the Montinola girls and their family. I missed them so much. I missed playing with them and their dachshund dogs, Hansel and Gretel.

"After my First Communion, I discovered that I really liked the taste of the host we'd receive during Mass on Sunday. Normally, I don't think I would have thought much about it, but given that we were hungry most of the time, it was a treat. It tasted great. There also seemed to be an endless supply of them. Every Sunday you'd see a heaping mound of them in the chalice on the altar.

"I was a pretty gutsy kid in those days, and if the other kids would dare me to do something, I usually did it. Well, one day I was talking about the host and how good it tasted, and some of the kids dared me to steal some. They rationalized that nobody would notice if just a few were missing from the chalice, and it seemed like there were too many to count. I went to the tent church and, when I saw that no one was looking, I ran up to the altar, grabbed the chalice, made a pocket with the front of my dress and dumped almost every one of the hosts into it. I quickly replaced the chalice, and ran at full speed back to the Annex. On the way, I noticed that I was being followed. I looked over my shoulder and saw about a dozen of the other children in the camp running after me! I quickly stuffed a handful of the hosts into my mouth and began chewing as quickly as I could. I let some drop to the ground, thinking that maybe I could get some of the kids to stop and pick them up. When I got back to the Annex, I had only a fraction of the hosts left in my dress and one very, very dry mouth!"

Jean-Marie was quickly getting a reputation among the Japanese guards as quite a little bundle of energy and spunk. She made them laugh. One guard in particular took a liking to Jean-Marie. He'd see her every day and would greet her with a wide smile. He was fascinated by the blonde curls on her head. She reminded him of a child film star that had become very popular in the United States.

"He was a younger guard than most of them, and he'd always smile and say, 'Ahh, Shelly Temple!' whenever he'd see me. When the other guards weren't listening, he'd tell me that he wanted to visit the United States someday when the war was over. He wanted to learn English, so I made him a deal. I would teach him how to speak English if he'd teach me how to speak Japanese. He readily agreed, and we would have our 'language classes' almost every day.

"One night we heard a knock on our room door, and we were surprised to hear that there were Japanese guards who wanted to see my mother and me outside of our room. I began to worry right away, because I was such a mischievous kid. I was probably in trouble for something I'd done. When we got out to the hallway, though, I saw the guard that called me 'Shelly Temple' standing with a couple of other guards. He smiled when he saw me, then he bowed and handed me a tin box filled with candy-coated almonds. I thanked him and bowed back, and I'll never forget the look on his face at that moment. His eyes were filled with so much sadness. He said to me, 'Jerry-san, me go to Bataan. No more come back.' Then he bowed again and left, and my mother and I returned to our room.

"Mom made me share the candy with all of the other children in the room. I never saw the guard again, and I can't recall his name. But I never forgot his kindness, or the sadness in his eyes."

During his years in Shanghai, Gene Faggiano had acquired a taste for the ancient and noble Chinese art of kite flying. Gene had a large collection of beautiful kites. There were fish kites, dragon kites, bird kites, butterfly and insect kites, squid kites, and others that were in the shape of mythical monsters from the vast store of Chinese folklore. Gene had learned how to build his own, and had eventually become so expert in their construction that his kites were among the best to be had anywhere. He knew all about their aerodynamics; how to balance them and what kind of paper would give them a certain kind of flight. He knew how to build kites for strong windy days, and how to build kites that needed no more than the gentlest of breezes.

Gene had also learned the art of kite fighting. Instead of using normal string, he would use a type of string made especially for this sport. The string was coated with tiny filaments of ground glass. Opposing players would try to maneuver their kites into a position that could cut the string of their adversary. These "dogfights" could go on for hours, and Gene became one of the best of the Shanghai kite flyers.

During that first year at Santo Tomas, Gene had somehow managed to find enough rice paper to build a kite. He spent his evenings gluing the feather-weight frame together and reinforcing it with pieces of thread. When he was finished, he painted it to look like a white crane with spreading wings. Followed by many of the children in the camp, Gene had taken Jean-Marie and Jimmy out to the baseball field to fly the new kite. As the kite gained altitude, children, internees, and even some of the Japanese guards, gathered on the baseball field to watch the marvelous white crane ride the thermals and updrafts. Gene had used his "razor string," a ball of which he had taken into the camp when they had been interned, thinking that someday he would find a use for it. After the crane had gained a good deal of height, an amazing thing happened. A blue butterfly kite, its string descending somewhere into the Filipino quarter across the street from the main gate, had soared into the air to challenge the white crane! Gene was an expert, but he had met his match with the invisible and unknown owner of the blue butterfly.

"Everyone watched the kite fight. Internees and guards alike, people momentarily forgot their roles as we mingled on the baseball diamond and watched the two kites dueling for supremacy in the air over Manila. Finally, Dad's kite took a vicious swoop into the blue butterfly, severing the anonymous owner's string. A cheer went up as the blue butterfly began spiraling down to defeat. Jimmy and I were so proud of Dad that day that we could have burst. Everyone was clapping him on the back and congratulating him. He was the man of the hour."

Eileen Faggiano was knitting one afternoon when she felt a tingling sensation on her left ankle. When she looked down, she saw a mosquito perched on her skin, ready to begin its blood-drawing ritual.

Eileen was keenly aware of the many sicknesses that existed in the camp. There were too many to count. She worried daily about her children and her husband. It was enough to keep the scrapes and bruises taken care of in less than sanitary conditions, but there were other things happening to internees that were far more serious. Many of the sick were suffering from a catalog of illnesses that accompanied malnutrition, including beri-beri, scurvy, salmonella, and dysentery. Internees suffered from intestinal parasites, hookworm, rheumatic fever, and hepatitis. And, of course, the diseases carried by mosquitoes. Malaria was a given. Everyone had it. It seemed not one pair of eyes in the camp had white in them anymore.

Then there was dengue fever.

On the afternoon that Eileen slapped away the mosquito that bit her left ankle, she didn't think much about it at first. She was fairly certain that she had swatted it off of her skin before the bite took a full hold. Later that afternoon, however, she began noticing symptoms in her body that began to frighten her. She had heard about dengue fever and knew that it had a nickname, "break-bone fever," for a reason.

"Mom first complained of having a mild fever, and thought maybe she had a slight viral infection or something. She thought it would pass, but the next thing we knew she started developing a severe headache, along with a bright red rash that started on her legs and then spread to the rest of her body. We took her to the camp hospital and the doctor diagnosed her with dengue fever.

"Mom had been in the hospital for a couple of days when the fever started getting worse. She looked terrible. She was shaking from severe pain all over her body. The doctor spoke with Dad, Jimmy, and me, and told us that she might be suffering from dengue shock syndrome, which could be fatal. That evening, Dad, Jimmy, and I said our prayers for Mom. We knew that if anyone was tough enough to pull out of this, Mom would.

"When we came to visit her the next day, we were horrified to find that her cot was near the 'death door.' The hospital staff kept those unlikely to survive near the entrance to the morgue as a matter of convenience. You could tell how far gone someone was by how close to the door they were placed. Mom's cot was three cots away from the door.

"Mom turned her head when she saw us come in the room. She saw the look in our eyes, and immediately gave us a stern look back. She said, 'Now you listen to me, all three of you, and listen good. I will survive this thing, by God. But I need every bit of strength to do it, and having you three moping around and feeling sorry for me isn't going to help.'

"Knowing my mother as well as I did, I knew that she was right. I also knew that somehow, someway, she would make it. She was determined to live, and she was going to show the doctors, the nurses, Dad, Jimmy, me, and even God Himself, that she would. That's the kind of woman my mother was. When she set her mind to do something, watch out. She was just that determined.

"After a few days, the nurses moved her away from the door. Her condition began to improve. Her pain, fever, and rashes began to disappear. Dad brought us to the hospital to help her leave. Typically, a person who had endured that kind of illness and had been that close to death would be bedridden for another day or so, at least. But Mom walked out of the hospital that day, and the doctors and nurses just shook their heads in disbelief. She knew she'd won the fight."

In November of 1943, shortly after Eileen's bout with dengue fever, a devastating typhoon struck the Philippines. With it came the rainfall, and plenty of it. Many of the shanties were destroyed, including the Faggiano's. The damage from the winds took out the electrical wiring and power, and the flooding caused contamination of the water supply. The deep water made it difficult to disseminate food and supplies. Many internees were forced to stay inside the buildings until the water levels dropped. After the waters subsided, the internees were faced with a massive cleanup and repair of the camp. The cleanup and repair effort took months to complete.

"It rained for days, and there was water and mud everywhere. The flooding was really bad. It had to have been at least two feet deep. We had just moved into a shanty in one of the courtyards of the Main Building for temporary housing until we could be moved into the Annex. When I had my tonsils removed a year before, they were put in a glass jar by Dr. Fletcher. My mother had them in a box that she kept in our shanty. I don't know how it happened, but somehow that glass jar with my tonsils ended up floating away, and we never did find them. My dad laughed and told me, 'Well, kiddo, they'll probably end up back in the States before we do…'"

The camp was getting crowded as more internees arrived over the course of the first couple of years. Many internees were moved to Los Banos, another internment camp thirty miles southeast of Manila. Los Banos had been set up in mid-1943 to handle the overflow from Santo Tomas and the population of several small, scattered internment camps further north. The first convoy of prisoners from Santo Tomas had been a group of 850 men between the ages of eighteen and forty. Some three hundred of them were volunteers. The rest had been "volunteered."

It was said that the conditions at Los Banos Internment Camp were similar to the conditions at Santo Tomas. The biggest difference between the two was that Santo Tomas was surrounded by a major city, while Los Banos was out in the country. Each of the internees had to decide for themselves which camp was preferable, weighing the pros and cons of each place, and the relative benefits of the two situations. Making the university livable had been a major project at Santo Tomas and, for a majority of the internees, leaving it now for points unknown seemed absurd and dangerously naive. The overwhelming majority of the Santo Tomas internee population preferred to remain in Santo Tomas, on the principle that the devil you know is better than the one you don't.

Gene's good friend, Jack Cassidy, made the decision to volunteer and go to Los Banos. Jack was a bachelor and on his own. He had no blood ties to hold him to Santo Tomas. The goodbye was awkward. Jack was best friends with Gene, and he was close to Eileen, Jimmy, and Jean-Marie as well. They said their farewells and wished each other the best of luck, promising that they'd reunite when this whole thing was over and have a huge celebration party at the St. Francis in San Francisco.

"The Red Cross had made arrangements with the Japanese to let the prisoners record a message that they could send home to their relatives. Internees were to let their families know that they were okay, that everything was fine and that the Japanese were treating them very well. The recording would be put on a phonograph record. It was all supposed to be positive or the record wouldn't go out. My mother made a recording for her grandmother in Baltimore, Maryland. In the recording, she talked about Dad, Jimmy, and me, and how we were being treated great by the Japanese and how we were really enjoying our stay. Then, at the end of the recording, she signed off with '...and tell it to the Marines!' This was an expression widely known among Americans as meaning 'don't believe a word of it.' The Japanese translators, unfamiliar with the expression, let it pass."

Eileen had sewn an apron for Jean-Marie in the first few months of their internment. On it were sewn a number of important dates, including the day the family entered Santo Tomas, Jean-Marie's First Communion, and Jean-Marie's tonsillectomy date. Eileen recorded these events in stitches using scrounged scraps of multicolored thread, intentionally leaving room on the apron for two more dates, and both were in the future. One was the date of their liberation. The other was the date that they would see the Golden Gate Bridge and step onto American soil.

"That first year at Santo Tomas was a time of adaption and change. We were told on the first day to bring enough clothes for three days. Well, it didn't take us long to figure out that we were going to be staying for a lot more than three days. We were just making the best of the situation, figuring that the war had to come to an end soon and we'd all be liberated and could go home. Hope is a powerful thing. You learned quickly to never talk about things in a negative way, even if you felt it inside. Every once in a while a 'bad thing' would happen to somebody, like the three Australian men who climbed the wall and escaped on the 12th of February of that first year. We heard that they were caught and executed by the Japanese three days later. You would see things and hear things that would invoke fear in your heart, but you learned to push past it. You kept busy. Life went on, and we just kept our hope up that it would all be over soon and life would get back to normal again.

"There were plenty of rumors running through the camp. One rumor we heard was that MacArthur was going to return 'in the next few days' and we would all be free again. Other rumors were not so positive. You'd hear that the Japanese had just bombed an American city or something like that. Any way you looked at it, rumors tended to create either false hopes or unnecessary fears, and that didn't serve anyone well.

"One thing that I liked to think about was the ice cream shop that my grandmother owned in the United States. I couldn't wait to visit someday... I had never met my grandmother, so the thought of meeting her for the first time was very exciting to me. What really got me excited, though, was thinking about all of that ice cream! Her shop was in San Rafael, California, and Dad told me that when we'd visit grandmother we'd see a big city called San Francisco and the Golden Gate Bridge, too. I used to daydream frequently about the day we'd arrive in California and visit grandmother's store. I fantasized about eating an ice cream sundae as tall as the clock tower at Santo Tomas. When I'd think about these things, I'd forget where I was for awhile. Daydreaming about my grandmother's store became one of my favorite pastimes.

"Toward the end of our second year of captivity, we began noticing that things in the camp were changing for the worse. We could sense a tension in the air with the Japanese. Something was happening in the world outside the gates of Santo Tomas that wasn't making them happy. The Japanese military was now in charge of the camp, and the civilian Japanese were gone. The list of rules became longer and stricter, and punishments became more severe and frequent. Food supplies became even more of a problem, and were getting progressively worse. By the end of that second year, most of our energy was spent trying to raise food or working on projects that the commandant declared as mandatory."

By 1944, the only thing left to do for the internees of Santo Tomas was to survive.

For the first time, Jean-Marie Faggiano began to wonder if things were really going to be all right after all.

Chapter Three

1944

As the internees at Santo Tomas entered their third year of captivity, their so-called "three day stay" had turned into a living nightmare. Although many internees suffered from a range of sickness and disease, including dysentery, dengue fever, and beriberi, their biggest problem by far was food. During the first six months of internment the Japanese had provided no food at all for the maintenance of the camp population. For their daily survival, all internees had to rely on packages and presents from friends or relatives from the outside. Every day, hundreds of Filipinos would assemble outside the main gate to present their packages for inspection and to wave at interned family members. The lines at the main gate quickly grew to what the authorities considered embarrassing proportions. On some days, almost a thousand people would be crowded outside on the street, waiting for a chance to make a donation to the internees. Some of these people didn't actually know anyone inside the camp. Risking the anger of the Japanese authorities, they came to help the internees as a matter of principle, and to flaunt a silent protest in the face of their conquerors.

"That first year, the Montinola family would bring us food that we knew they couldn't afford to give up. Times were tough outside the camp, too, and the Montinola family had a large family to feed. They unselfishly took from their own food supplies to make sure we had something to eat. They were the kindest and most caring people we ever knew."

By mid-1942, a Red Cross commission had been set up in Tokyo under the auspices of the Swiss embassy. Using this newly formed diplomatic channel, the American and Canadian chapters of the Red Cross had been able to ship food, clothes, and medical supplies for the use of American civilian and military POWs. The Japanese, however, made it clear that any allotment of supplies permitted inside the camp for the internees would depend on how charitable they happened to feel toward the prisoners at the moment. The population of the camp could be punished or rewarded by food, or lack of food, at any given time; a weapon far more effective than bayonets or barbed wire.

Each new American advance in the Pacific had the immediate effect of reducing rations, not only Santo Tomas, but at every prison, slave labor, and internment camp from Borneo to Shanghai. In places where conditions were far worse than at Santo Tomas -- on the Thai-Burmese railway, at Fort Santiago, at Bilibid Prison, or at Cabanatuan -- even a tiny reduction in rations could mean a death sentence.

In August of 1944, Santo Tomas received a new commandant, Lieutenant Colonel Toshio Hayashi. Hayashi announced that due to circumstances beyond their control, the Japanese army could no longer guarantee adequate shipments of food for the camp. Therefore, in the future, all internees would be required to produce enough food from their garden plot to feed themselves and their families. This announcement caused a wave of alarm through the camp. It was clearly impossible to live off the tiny patch of unproductive ground allotted to each prisoner.

Jean-Marie could remember a time in the past when she always had enough to eat. By the summer of 1944, however, these were just memories that no longer had the power to generate any sense of reality. Good food, and all you could eat, belonged in the same realm of fantasy as fairy tales or rumors of liberation. The reality was that Jean-Marie, like the rest of the camp population, was getting weaker by the day. Jean-Marie was prone to dizzy spells. Her mouth was full of sores and her taste buds had died away. Her stomach had shriveled up, and there was almost no flesh left on her arms and legs. She knew that somewhere, people had enough to eat and some day, somehow, someone was supposed to come and liberate them so that they, too, would have enough to eat. But for right now, all she could think about was food and how to get it. It seemed that was all anybody ever thought about, talked about, or dreamed about.

"We used to eat together as a family in the early days of the camp. As time went on, however, it had become almost impossible to be served at the same time and eat together. Dad had an early morning work assignment, and Mom had her room monitor duties. Often times, Jimmy and I ended up eating with other kids who were pretty much in the same predicament with their parents.

"Every day we would line up for meals from the kitchen, holding our tin cans and plates, homemade bamboo spoons, and the precious cardboard meal ticket. You guarded that meal ticket with your life, because without it you couldn't eat. Our meals usually consisted of a half cup of lugao, which is a rice paste, and a cup of coconut milk. At our house on Del Pilar, before our internment, Anselma Lusardi would use lugao to paste pictures and postcards on the black pages of our photo album. Now it was a main source of food in our diet.

"In the early days of the camp, we used sifters to sift out the bugs that would end up in our rice. As time went on, however, we just left them in. Dr. Fletcher had told us that the bugs were actually a good source of protein.

"There were a number of animals in the camp in the beginning, like chickens, ducks, and hogs, but most were gone by end of the second year. During our first year of internment we did manage to get this white rooster, a small, thin bird that had a cancerous growth on its neck and face area. Dad decided that we might as well eat the bird, even if it was cancerous. Mom, Jimmy, and I were concerned that we'd end up getting what the rooster had, but he assured us we'd be fine. Dad used his trusty Gillette blade and cut the little rooster's head off. Who cared if it had cancer? It tasted wonderful. Mom deep fried it, using cold cream from a Red Cross package.

"Around the second year of our internment we had planted a fairly nice vegetable garden. The Japanese had actually given us the seeds to plant the garden. Once the garden grew, however, they came in and picked all of the vegetables for themselves, except for the garlic. If we were left anything, I suppose garlic was a good choice. It wasn't the easiest to eat, but it did help keep the worms out of your system. Mom told me that intestinal worms will eat everything you eat. This means that you'd always be hungry and would eventually die from starvation, even though you were eating. Knowing this, suddenly the garlic didn't taste so bad.

"The few dogs and cats that used to roam the camp disappeared over time, as did the flocks of pigeons that used to roost in the overhanging eaves of the camp buildings. Any other time, the thought that someone had used them for food would've sickened me, but when you are faced with starvation, you don't question the source of any meat that ends up in your meal. If you get it, you eat it. And gratefully.

"During the previous two years, there had been more food and more hope to go around. There used to be a pleasant sense of camaraderie at breakfast; you'd hear far-fetched rumors, camp politics, jokes, and light, early morning banter. People could reserve a place in line by leaving a stool or having a friend stand in for them. There had even been music over the loudspeakers. Now, though, it was a different story. There were more fights and confrontations. Everybody's nerves were stretched to the breaking point, and old resentments and animosities were bubbling to the surface. Every meal was a gloomy affair, with former friends and neighbors watching each other like hawks to make sure that they got as much, or as little, as the next person.

"If I was lucky enough to get in line before most, I'd have time in the morning to eat my lugao, clean my tin can with sand, and head back to the kitchen. Some of the other kids would join me. We would duck under the serving table, where hundreds of internees would still be waiting in line, and we would scrape the underside of the table for any stray scraps that might have fallen between the cracks. Then we'd check the dirt under the table. Sometimes you'd find a lump of lugao or a grain of yesterday's rice. Sometimes you'd find nothing.

"When we searched for food like this in the beginning, some of the adults would joke with us, or express sympathy for the harsh circumstances of the children. But that soon changed. We could feel the increasing resentment from the adults, as hunger wore away at compassion. We learned to ignore the angry shouts and threats. Of course, as kids, we would also have problems amongst ourselves. We were out for number one, and it became a game of 'finders, keepers.' Many times we'd get into a fistfight over who spotted the morsel in the dirt first."

Jean-Marie had a special friend that worked in the camp kitchen. His name was Pendleton Thompson, but his nickname was "Bumblebee," and that's what he liked to be called. Bumblebee was one of the few black men in the camp. He was usually in the kitchen dealing with the heavy vats of rice mush when Jean-Marie would see him, and he always had a smile and a greeting for her.

"Bumblebee was the nicest man around. He always greeted everyone with a cheerful hello, every day. If you asked him how he was, he'd always answer with, 'Deeeeelightful!' He seemed to possess an endless spiritual and physical reserve of steady strength. He lost a lot of weight, just like all of us, but he still seemed big. Every time he'd see me he'd say, 'Good morning, Jerry-san! How are you?' He knew my nickname, Jerry, and he added the 'san' at the end, just to mimic the Japanese, which always made me laugh.

"On special occasions, like my First Communion or birthday, Bumblebee would take me aside and secretly hand me a smuggled coconut candy or a surprise rice cake. He did this for a lot of the children in the camp. He was a skilled cook, and I had heard that before the war he cooked for a steamship line, much like the one that Dad worked for. His skills in the kitchen were of immediate and critical use, and he was well respected.

"Whenever you saw Bumblebee, you immediately felt hope. He could cheer you up out of the darkest of moods. He had such a sense of humor, poise, and self-confidence. He made everyone around him feel better. For me, he was larger than life. He loved kids and would go out of his way to make us smile."

Jean-Marie also held a deep respect for a young, pretty girl named Moira Malone. Moira was the envy of most of the girls and women in the camp, and was certainly considered the camp sweetheart. She was from England, and Jean-Marie thought she had to be one of the most beautiful girls in the world.

"Moira's hair was long, black, and shiny... she used to wash her hair every day with gogo bark. She had beautiful skin and bright blue eyes. Everything about her was soft and graceful, even in her current emaciated condition. All the young men were crazy about her."

At the beginning of their internment, Eileen Faggiano was the room monitor of Room 48 in the Main Building. Her responsibility was to ensure that everyone was in place and accounted for during the twice daily roll call, and to make sure the rooms were kept as orderly as possible. And, of course, she would hand out the five squares of toilet paper to each person in her room every morning. In mid-1943, Eileen and Jean-Marie had been moved to the Annex, a single story building behind the Main Building. Because of her previous experience as room monitor in the Main Building, Eileen was a natural choice as room monitor for their new dwelling. The

Annex rooms were smaller than the Main Building rooms, and housed about twenty-five women and children per room.

One morning, during a routine roll call, Eileen was about to experience firsthand the effects of the change of camp leadership. The new commandant, Lieutenant Colonel Toshio Hayashi, was the most feared of all the commandants the internees had lived under. He was in his late forties and was Imperial Japanese Army to the core. As Jean-Marie's father would say, he was "a real son of a bitch."

According to Jean-Marie, on this particular morning Hayashi sent his right hand man, another feared officer, Lieutenant Abiko, to the Annex to perform an inspection and take roll call. Eileen assembled the whole room outside their door in the hallway, standing at attention. One of the guards was beginning to make notes on his clipboard as the lieutenant approached the row of internees. As Abiko walked down the line, each internee bowed from the waist as he passed.

"I was standing next to Mom when I heard a razzing noise from one of the children. There was an awful prolonged silence, and then Lieutenant Abiko suddenly was standing in front of my mother. As she straightened from her bow, he slapped her very hard across the face. It echoed in the room. Abiko then pointed his finger at a little boy, who couldn't have been more than two or three years old.

"The boy hadn't bowed. He continued making razzing noises with his mouth. It was if the child was giving Abiko a Bronx cheer.

"They marched Mom down the hallway and into the middle section of the Annex, to an area away from our eyes. We had to continue standing at attention in the hallway, so we couldn't see what was happening to her. We could, however, hear the angry shouts, followed by slaps and my mother's cries. All of us were frightened for her, and there was absolutely nothing we could do.

"After what seemed like an eternity, Mom came back into the hallway. Her face was red and puffy, and her left eye was blackened and swollen shut. Her mouth and nose were bleeding and her hair was messed up. She looked terrible. We immediately came out of attention and gathered around her, but she waved us off, not wanting any sympathy. She dabbed at her busted lip with the sleeve of her already bloodied blouse and said to us, 'We need to make sure... that this little boy learns... how to bow... and learns it... before the next roll call tonight. I suggest... we start now.'

"For the remainder of that morning, afternoon, and up to the evening roll call, we rehearsed the bow with the little boy. When Abiko and his men returned that evening, that little child bowed correctly and didn't finish bowing until the lieutenant had passed him in the line. And, of course, the kid never made a peep. No Bronx cheer this round. When Abiko left after the evening roll call, there was a huge release of air from everyone's lungs. We were all holding our breath."

Jean-Marie's father had a permanent job in the camp for which he was paid in a daily allotment of camote tops. Gene would spend six hours a day, six days a week, rolling a large cart of food supplies from the bodega to the kitchen and back again, over and over. Gene missed his good friend, Jack Cassidy, who left for Los Banos the year before. Jack was his partner in the cart work assignment from the front gate to the bodega, but since Jack's departure, Gene got help from whoever had the assignment that week. While Gene and his partner rolled the cart from the kitchen to the bodega, they had to keep an eye on the load and watch for hijackers. This was a different time than when he and Jack rolled the cart. Now, teenage internees, made bold by gnawing hunger, had been forming gangs that would swoop down on a load and run off with whatever they could grab. A load of bananas or rice was like a load of gold bullion, and it would be carefully checked and tallied by Japanese officials on both ends of its short journey. Gene and his partner would be held responsible for any missing food, but there were always scraps, or a leak in a sack of rice, that gave Gene an opportunity to pass Jean-Marie and Jimmy a mouthful of extra food. It had gotten harder to pull this off as the daily rations dropped. Hundreds of eyes could be following the progress of the cart across the grounds. One informer would be all it would take. Everyone knew the score. Principals and community spirit were all steadily eroding under the weight of famine.

"One day I went to see my dad while he was working. He was pulling the cart and another man was pushing. I don't know why, but for some reason when I saw him from the distance, I suddenly had this flash in my mind of Dad before the war. He was such a good looking man, a talented all-around athlete. Boxing had been his strongest sport, and he could make a punching bag fly at incredible rates of speed. My brother and I used to sit amazed as he'd hit the bag with lightning speed, using both fists and elbows, keeping perfect rhythm. He was an avid golfer, amateur photographer, fanatic Jai Alai, football, and baseball fan.

"That afternoon, I flashed back to an evening when I saw him dressed 'to the nines,' ready to take my mother out to a night on the town. He was standing on the porch of our house on Del Pilar, waiting for Mom to finish dressing. He had been so handsome in his snow white dinner jacket, white linen shirt, and black bow tie. He was my dad, and he looked like a movie star.

"The man I was looking at this day, however, didn't look anything like the person with the white dinner jacket. Pulling the creaking cart toward me, his face was drawn and haggard. His skin was stretched thin over his cheekbones. He was dressed in ragged, patched khaki shorts and wooden bakyas. Every bone in his body was visible. His legs were swollen with beriberi and covered with sores. And suddenly I could feel the tears sting my eyes. I started to shake, and I just started crying. Even though I had seen him every day since we arrived at the camp, for some reason his appearance that afternoon just hit me like a ton of bricks.

"That day, I just waved at my father from a distance, because I didn't want him to worry if he saw tears in my eyes. He looked up, a gaunt stick figure of a man, and when he saw me he waved and smiled that smile of his that could light up even the darkest room. I waved back and acted like I had to run off and do something else. I found a place behind the Annex where no one was looking, and I cried until I couldn't cry anymore."

Jean-Marie learned quickly that there really weren't many places to hide in an internment camp. This was a place where doors, especially doors with locks, huts with more than two walls, bathroom partitions, showers, private possessions, and cohabitation of man and wife, were all illegal. Privacy in any form was expressly forbidden by the Japanese. The first law an internee would have to learn was, "If you want privacy, close your eyes."

"I remember in the beginning many internees were complaining of the lack of privacy. You couldn't do anything without being visible to someone. After awhile, though, modesty fades away as you get acclimated to the situation, and you realize that everybody else has the same problem with privacy, too. I'm not sure who it was that came up with the saying, 'If you want privacy, close your eyes,' but it was pretty much true. Often times we would take a nap during the day, and even if I wasn't tired, just closing my eyes seemed to take me into my own little private space for awhile.

"During the monsoons, I used to like to go to the wood shed and lay down on the planks of the crawl space. It was a storage area for lumber, most of which had been used up, so the space was usually empty. I liked it because it was dry and dark under the shed. The crawl space was elevated a good yard off the ground to keep the lumber, when there was any, from being ruined during the rainy season. When I had nothing better to do during the monsoon, I would lie on the planks and watch the rain and the lightning. I had a game that I liked to play when I was all alone. I would lie on my favorite spot where there was a wide crack between two boards. I'd look though the crack and watch the water flowing along the ground beneath me. Every once in a while, a snake would slither by, or a big frog would make an appearance. I knew there were people in camp who caught the frogs and snakes to eat, but I didn't know how anyone could eat anything so slimy. Sometimes, I would pretend that I was an angel looking down from heaven on the wide oceans of the world, or I would just let my mind drift and create fantasies of the world outside the barbed-wire walls."

One of Jean-Marie's favorite things to do during the monsoons was to watch the mud fish. The mud fish never failed to be entertaining. During the dry season they lived a foot beneath the surface of the hard baked ground in suspended animation. When the monsoons came, however, the soil would loosen sufficiently and the strange catfish look-alikes would rise to the surface to mate and hunt for food.

Many of the camp children passed the time by playing with beetles that were often found in the camp. These beetles were called salagubangs. They were large and black, with a hard glossy shell, long, sensitive feelers, and huge, serrated jaws.

"I had a pet salagubang that I named Sally. She was the only pet I could have in the camp... all of the cats and dogs and other animals were gone by that third year. I think every child in the camp had, at one time or another, their own pet salagubang. I would tie one end of a light piece of string to one of Sally's legs, and the other end to a button or a hole in my clothes. Sally would sometimes sit on my shoulder or she would crawl around my neck and back. Once in a while she would take off flying, but because she was tethered to me, she couldn't fly away. She'd end up flying in circles around me until she got tired of that, and then she'd land on me again and eventually end up back on my shoulder. I used to put grass or tiny bugs on my shoulder for Sally to eat.

"One of the funny things about Sally was that she reminded me of Hernando, our pet cockatoo at our house on Del Pilar. Hernando would try to fly sometimes, and forget that his leg was tied to the end of the perch. He would end up flying in a circle, just like Sally. Hernando liked flying after things, too. He loved Dad's spaghetti, and would sometimes fly into it if he wasn't tethered. One time, Mom had a bunch of her high society friends over for tea, including the wealthy cosmetics lady, Helena Rubinstein. Ms. Rubinstein's hair was pulled up on her head in a fancy hairdo, and Hernando wasn't tied to his perch that particular day. I guess the hairdo reminded him of spaghetti. He made a beeline for her head, and she screamed and almost fainted right then and there. That was the last time Helena Rubinstein ever came to our house. Whenever I had Sally flying around on a string, I'd often think of that wacky bird and his attack on Ms. Rubinstein's hairdo."

For the children in the camp, games became a common, everyday occurrence. Jean-Marie enjoyed playing marbles with her friends, and jumping rope was just as fun. Her father taught her how to skip rope, something Gene did quite a bit of while training as a boxer. Before they were interned, Gene gave Jean-Marie her first set of marbles, and she had brought them with her to the camp.

"Dad was very competitive and he taught Jimmy and me that if we play, then we should to play to win. Sometimes, however, I would take that too far end up getting in a fight with some poor kid. I was pretty feisty in those days."

Playing "pretend" was always fun, too. Many of the camp's children fantasized themselves in a world far apart from the dire circumstances they woke up to daily. They were suddenly kings, queens, medieval knights and princesses. And, of course, there was the all-American classic game of pretend: "Cowboys and Indians."

Jimmy Faggiano and his friends were involved in a "Cowboys and Indians" game one afternoon. In preparation for his role as Indian Chief, Jimmy had spent several days working on a bamboo bow-and-arrow set. He diligently scrounged up the bamboo slats, found a piece of string, cut a few arrowheads out of tin cans, and sharpened them against the concrete steps of the Education Building. On the big day, just as the fury of the cowboy attack on the Indian war party had reached its peak, Jean-Marie had made the mistake of wandering across the field of glory on her way to play dolls with her friends, unaware of the carnage all around her. Jimmy, excited, acted on impulse and sent an arrow flying in her general direction.

"I was walking along when suddenly something hit the back of my head with a 'thwack!' I reached my hand up and there was this arrow stuck in my head. Jimmy dropped his bow and arrow and just stared at me in dazed horror. I yelled, 'Now you're gonna' get it! I'm telling!' As I ran for the Annex to tell Mom, Jimmy ran after me and tried to talk me out of it, but I ignored him."

Cowboys and Indians scattered in all directions. Internees stopped in amazement at the sight of this little girl, running across campus with an arrow sticking straight out of the back of her head, with a dark blood stain spreading down the collar of her dress.

"Mom pulled the rusty tin arrowhead gently from my head and washed the wound in cold water. Then she started swearing up a storm. She said to me, 'First, I'm going to take care of you, and then I'm going to find "Geronimo"... and when I do, I'm going to kill him!' Well, Mom did find Jimmy, but she never killed him. He did get a pretty good spanking though, and a verbal tongue lashing from both Mom and Dad."

One of Jean-Marie's favorite people in the camp was an elderly British lady named Mrs. Boycott. She taught Jean-Marie how to knit and crochet, using bamboo needles made by Jean-Marie's father. Mrs. Boycott would use the same skein of heavy woolen yarn over and over again, and would pass the time by knitting a pair of socks, unraveling them every few hours, and then knitting them over again in a different pattern. It didn't bother her that she had to constantly undo them each time. In the Philippines, even in the winter months, no one would want a heavy pair of woolen socks anyway.

"Mrs. Boycott loved to play a game she fondly called the 'Recipe Game.' She would see me sometimes and wave me over to her, where she'd then reach into her pocket and pull out a small slip of white paper and a yellow pencil stub. She'd then ask me, 'What shall we make today, sweetheart? How about a nice chocolate cake?' and I'd nod enthusiastically. More of the children would gather around her as she'd explain how the cake was made. Mrs. Boycott never left out any details. As she reeled off the ingredients, each one a delicacy by itself, she would help me write it down on her slip of paper. When the game was over, the recipe would be erased and the precious slip of paper would be ready to go again.

"The 'Recipe Game' was bittersweet. On one hand, it seemed crazy talking about something as delicious as chocolate cake when you're hungry all the time. On the other hand, as funny as this might sound, once the recipe game was finished, you somehow felt a bit... well, satisfied. It was a strange sensation, and it started catching on in the camp. Some folks couldn't be bothered with it, discounting it as a fool's game. I always felt better after I played it, though, especially when Mrs. Boycott would describe the ingredients like she would with her British accent."

"Jimmy and I would sometimes do our own version of the 'Recipe Game,' only we'd pretend we were making our own ice cream sundaes at Grandmother's ice cream store in California. Jimmy would start with chocolate ice cream, his favorite. I began with vanilla, my favorite. Then the fun would really start. We'd begin adding syrups, whipped cream, candies galore, and sprinkles of this or that. Pretty soon, our ice cream sundaes were as high as the ceiling! I came back to Mrs. Boycott one afternoon and told her about our ice cream recipes, and she laughed out loud. She said, 'Child, you keep that thought in your head, because one day you and your brother are going to make those sundaes, just as you imagined them!'"

Jean-Marie and her friends were just outside of the Annex one afternoon, playing a game of hopscotch, when they spotted the woman who made everybody cringe. She was known as the "Camp Angel," a Filipino matron who drove her horse and cart into Santo Tomas to pick up the dead and take them to the nearby cemetery. Jean-Marie and her girlfriends used to play a game of trying to guess how many bodies were inside the covered funeral cart, based on how low it sat on its springs. On that day, the cart was almost sitting on its wheels, with the springs squeezed down to the maximum. The poor horse that was pulling the cart was exhausted from the extra weight.

"We were guessing at the body count, when suddenly the cart tipped backwards and a single body rolled out onto the road, releasing the springs. The horse shot forward with a lurch and almost threw the 'Camp Angel' from the cart. We recognized the dead woman; a heavyset, elderly lady who had gone to the hospital in the last week with beriberi. The sickness had bloated her up to enormous proportions. It took five men to hoist the woman's body back into the cart. As the cart creaked off on its way, the horse began to protest, and we began giggling. Then we resumed our game of hopscotch, as if nothing had happened.

"When I think back on that afternoon, I'm not proud to admit that we found something as tragic as the cart incident so amusing, but I also think of how many dead people we had seen since we arrived in the camp. That constant exposure to the dead and dying tends to desensitize you to things that would normally horrify you. And we were all silently aware that there was always room in that covered cart for us, too. Sometimes laughter is the only way to cope with that and still maintain your sanity."

The children of Santo Tomas had acquired a subtle feel for their tricky relationship with the Japanese. Much was permitted, but there were unexpected areas that could prove dangerous. The children traded information on the quirks and idiosyncrasies of each Japanese guard. They gave them nicknames, and did their best to assess whether each guard was a "good Jap"

or a "bad Jap." It was important not to make any mistakes on this point. Japanese customs and traditions, being largely unknown, often forced the children to find out what the limits were by trial and error.

For many of the children, the Japanese had become their main source of entertainment. They were always up to something new. One afternoon, Lieutenant Abiko had ordered his men to drill in the use of machine guns and bayonets. Abiko had his regiment of fifty or so guards in an attack drill, advancing across the former baseball diamond in the face of the imaginary enemy. Every few yards, the machine gunners would fling themselves down in the soft infield dust and pretend to sweep the area before them with machine gun fire. The children had found this hysterically funny, and packs of tiny internees had followed them, imitating their every move and shrieking with laughter. When the Japanese guards screamed "BANZAI!" and charged with leveled bayonets, the children were right at their heels. The game had gone on for hours. None of their parents were particularly worried by this. It had been demonstrated time and time again that most of the Japanese had a deep reverence and affection for small children, even the children of their military enemies. Small gifts were sometimes forthcoming, when the private soldier felt safe from the scrutiny of his superiors. Parents were held responsible for their children's strict observance of camp rules and regulations, but the children themselves were normally in no danger of punishment or reprisal. There were, however, sporadic lapses in this unwritten agreement by particularly brutal or fanatical guards, the "bad Japs." According to Jean-Marie's mother, Eileen, one of these guards had jabbed the tip of his bayonet into the calf of ten year old "Awful Albert" for something the boy did that angered him. As a rule, however, instances of deliberate brutality toward children were extremely rare. It can be argued that slow starvation behind prison walls is the ultimate brutality, but the individual guards had no control over the policies of the Tokyo government. It was a common sight to see some tough veteran of the Manchurian campaign giving piggyback rides to a giggling American toddler. Nor was it remarkable to see two guards patiently twirling a jump rope for an eager line of boys and girls.

"Most of the Japanese guards were nice to the children in the camp. My brother and I figured out a simple way to determine whether a Japanese guard was a 'good Jap' or a 'bad Jap.' We'd smile at them and watch how they reacted. If they smiled back, you knew they were okay. No problem. If they didn't smile back, however, we knew to avoid them as much as humanly possible, and spread a warning to the other kids, too. Jimmy and I learned that the 'bad Japs' were not to be fooled with."

But Jean-Marie would sometimes push her luck with the Japanese guards, especially if it involved the acquisition of food.

Or a dare from her brother.

"One day, Jimmy and I were watching one of the Japanese privates walking toward a work site with lunch for the other guards. From each of his hands dangled a heavy steel bucket, heaped with white rice. I could see the steam curling into the air behind the guard as he walked. The sight and smell of the rice was absolutely mesmerizing. Jimmy began daring me right away to steal some. This was an old game of his, and I knew it by heart. Even so, it still occasionally had the power to make me act. Whenever he wanted something he was afraid to get, he'd dare me to do it for him. It had worked over and over again. I'd never turn down a dare from him, and he knew it. This time, though, he was asking for the impossible. Jimmy kept daring me, but I hardly heard him. My stomach was growling and my mouth was watering. I just couldn't tear my eyes away from those white, steaming mounds of rice."

Jimmy could see from her expression that her will to resist was crumbling. But soon it would be too late. The guard with the rice buckets was getting closer to the work site. Jimmy, losing hope, used his trump card, the big gun.

He double dared her.

"... and the next thing I knew, my feet were carrying me toward the guard with the rice. I ran up to within a foot of him and plunged my hands into both buckets. It took a half second for me to realize that steaming rice meant very *hot* rice! The pain was excruciating. I scooped up two heaping handfuls and hugged them to my chest. The guard grunted in surprise, then shouted in anger. I spun and ran for my life in the direction of the women's Annex. The guard took off after me and almost caught me in the first few strides, but the buckets of rice were too much of a handicap. He didn't dare put them down and run after me. If he did, he knew that by the time he got back not a grain would be left, and he would be held responsible.

"When I finally arrived at the Annex, nobody was there. I hid under my cot, with tears of agony streaming down my face. I dumped the rice in the lap of my play dress and looked down at my hands. They were a solid mass of white blisters. I couldn't recall ever experiencing that kind of pain. I rocked back and forth, trying to make it go away. After a few minutes, the pain subsided and I started to devour the rice, making each life giving mouthful last as long as I could. I didn't save any for Jimmy. He could go get his own. I'd paid for it."

There were a few internees who had a way of knowing, with remarkable accuracy, what was happening in the world outside the camp. But only they knew the source of their information. To let anyone else know risked discovery from the Japanese, and if the Japanese found out, the consequences could be severe. Nonetheless, information gave you hope, especially if it was the kind of information that revealed progress in the war to the advantage of the Americans and their allies. It brought the hope of liberation closer.

What these men possessed were simple radios, hand-made crystal sets. At various times they had been hidden in varying, ingenious methods: a double-bottomed pressure cooker, or a false-bottomed three legged stool. The technique these men used to spread the news was to go to the latrines and pass the word along in the form of rumors, never giving any indication that the rumors were any different than those that had been running rampant since the first day the camp opened. In this way, they never let another internee know their secret. Apparently, these men didn't even know that the other men who had radios, had radios.

The Japanese began to notice the mysterious way that a percentage of the rumors running through the camp came very close to the truth of the war in the Pacific. In some cases, internees were heard to repeat to each other important developments in the fighting before the Japanese had heard of it. The guards had gone on numerous early morning rampages, tearing the rooms apart, searching in every conceivable location for the hidden radio they were certain was just waiting to be found. The dreaded *Kempeitai*, the military police arm of the Imperial Japanese Army, had interrogated more than a few internees who seemed to know more than they should.

After all of the searches and interrogations, the Japanese never found any of the radios. If they had, there certainly would've been at least one execution outside the gates of Santo Tomas.

Chapter Four

September 1944

Members of the former religious services committee posted a notice to all internees in response to the alarming breakdown of camp morale and morals. All religious activities had long ago been forbidden by the military police, but happily the Japanese censors had remained unaware that this form of document was inherently religious in nature.

Ten Commandments For Santo Tomas

1. Thou shalt have no other interest greater than the welfare of the camp.

2. Thou shalt not adopt for thyself, nor condone in others, any merely selfish rule of conduct, or indulge in any practice that injures the morale of the camp. Thou shalt not violate the procedures agreed upon by the authorities or the majority, for punishment will surely be visited upon all, innocent and guilty alike, because of the misdeeds of a few.

3. Thou shalt not betray the ideals and principals which thou wast taught, so that in the future thou wilt not be condemned for neglecting the heritage.

4. Remember the work of the camp to do thy share. Six days shall thou labor and do all thy work assignments, and also on thy rest day refresh thy mind and heart. For thy work will be satisfying and effective only when it is done in the right spirit.

5. Honor thy forefathers by recalling vividly their struggle for better things, that thou mayst contribute now and in the days to come to the realization of their ideals.

6. Thou shalt not hinder the best development of youth in the camp.

7. Thou shalt not break down family relationships.

8. Thou shalt not steal.

9. Thou shalt not injure thy neighbor's reputation by malicious gossip.

10. Thou shalt not covet thy neighbor's shanty or his room space. Thou shalt not covet thy neighbor's wife, or his fiancée, or his influential position, or anything that is thy neighbor's.

"I'll never forget the morning I woke up and saw one of the Muir girls, Bella, standing frozen in place and staring intently at the entrance to our room in the Annex. I turned over in my cot and looked towards the direction of her stare, and immediately felt the hair stand up on the back of my neck. A group of Japanese guards were standing in the doorway. By the looks on their faces, I could tell they were upset about something."

The entire room was now awake and staring at the guards in terrified expectation. Normally, everyone would all be getting out of bed at this hour, stretching, joking, complaining, gossiping, humming, arguing, scratching flea and bedbug bites, rolling up their netting, and getting in line for the bathroom. The sudden appearance of the guards had caught the room by complete surprise. Everyone came to their senses at once and bowed.

The guards marched over to Eileen and Jean-Marie.

"I thought about the two handfuls of rice, and I got an immediate sinking feeling in my stomach. I thought, 'Oh God, I'm a goner. They're going to chop my head off.' I was sure I was going to be led to the front gate. Instead, one of the guards picked up my teddy bear and looked my mother right in the eye. Mom had a five pound gold bar and assorted jewelry and coins hidden inside the teddy bear. They knew it and she knew they knew it. Mom stood there, trying to think of an answer, a solution, some way out. And then, just as quickly as they had entered the room, they marched out the door.

"Mom waited until she was sure that they had left the building. She then turned and looked at the woman in the next bunk. This was a woman that my mother always suspected was doing things for the Japanese. She asked the woman if it was her that tipped the Japanese about the teddy bear, and the woman refused to answer. I've never seen my mother so angry. She was furious. She started calling that woman names I'd never heard before. I thought Mom was going to hit her, but she never did. And that woman never said a word back... she just stood there and stared at the floor.

"I think the worst part of this whole ordeal was not so much my mother's fury, but the way the whole room now regarded this woman. Informers were considered cowards, traitors. The entire internee community was built on trust, and this was a clear infringement. Being a collaborator with the Japanese meant you were sometimes given certain favors, maybe food or special treatment or privileges. Being discovered as a collaborator by your fellow internees, however, was a sure way to risk hostilities and alienation from the rest of the camp."

As the news of this incident reached outside the Annex room, it would undoubtedly contribute to the already waning trust among the internees. There was an increasing breakdown in camp morale, and this morning's revelation would just fuel the fire. It would spread like a cancer through the camp. Hope and trust were two of the only things the internees had left to keep their spirits alive. Without one, the other was sure to collapse.

All over Santo Tomas, all over Manila, people froze in position as an air raid siren went off. The wailing of the sirens went on and on, but there was nothing to be seen in the sky. An entire population of people held their breath, listening for the roar of engines, the whistle of falling bombs. No engines, no bombs, nothing but clouds and flocks of birds. The sirens howled for half an hour more before falling away into silence.

At the first sound of the siren, Hayashi ordered the camp defenses on full alert. Guards sprinted in all directions, manning machine guns on the roofs of the Education and Main Buildings, taking position. It was the first excitement in a long time, and Hayashi's troops were avidly scanning the skies, longing for a target to blow to pieces. On the roof of every tall building in Manila, men were standing by with their weapons, staring at the sky through the grid of anti-aircraft gun sights. After the first rush of mindless motion, while the seconds, then the minutes, ticked away in silence, the guards of Santo Tomas and the multitudes of other Japanese soldiers of the Fourteenth Area Army stationed in Manila began to realize that the war had come home, a pulse beat away, pressing toward them like a vast tidal wave. The islands would be engulfed in fire. They were expected to fight to the last bullet, to the last drop of blood, to the last man. It's possible that the thought may have occurred to them that the internees -- triumphant, smiling, and celebrating -- might be liberated over their dead bodies.

Internees lined the windows of the buildings, standing motionless like ragged statues scattered across the campus. Hope was dawning for the first time in memory... real hope, not the vain repetition of wishful thoughts and slogans. A new born faith was rising out of the ashes of doubt, cynicism, and despair. It could happen. The day may really be at hand. It seemed too good to be true, too fraught with the peril of disappointment to even consider seriously. But they couldn't deny their own eyes and ears. Japanese officers were in their shelters. Guards stood ready with rifles and machine guns. For the internees, the sight of their warders crouched down on the earth, nervously waiting for the terrible retribution to come, was a feeling beyond the power of words to describe.

After the sirens finally died away, the internees found themselves laughing, slapping each other on the back, and filled with a nondiscriminatory feeling of fellowship they would not have believed possible an hour before. The main joke of the moment was the way the Japanese air defenses had started the alert with the "all clear" signal, and ended it with the "air raid warning." Women broke out secret caches of goodies stored carefully away over the months. Men felt the length of their beards and decided they could do with a trim. A current of hope began flowing through them. The sound of the sirens had given them a possible future.

All over the South Pacific, vast forces were wrapped in a death struggle in the "war without mercy." A million men were slogging through jungles, sweltering in caves, hunkered down on battleships, aircraft carriers, destroyers, opening bomb bay doors, bailing out of flaming fighters, being drowned or suffocated or burnt or blown apart or buried alive. Allied forces were suffering thousands of dead and tens of thousands of wounded to gain tiny coral atolls that were barely dots on the map. The Caroline Islands, Truk, Guadalcanal, the Gilberts, Midway, Tarawa, Yap. There were ammo ships going up in a single flash, raining unexploded shells on friend and foe in a circumference of death a dozen miles wide. There were wounded submarines, filled with screaming, terrified men, leaking air and settling slowly into deep, black ocean trenches. Entire landscapes transformed overnight by the massive pounding of sixteen inch naval gunfire.

The Pacific war presented a rolling ocean wave of fire and terror, the likes of which the world had never seen or imagined. Japanese losses were staggering. On island after island, cut off, without hope of reinforcement or victory, they fought with maniacal, suicidal fury, until they were utterly exterminated. Neither side bothered to take many prisoners.

For months, MacArthur had been embroiled in a bitter feud with the allied high command and the Joint Chiefs of Staff. The overwhelming majority opinion was against him, favoring a direct strike at Formosa, thereby establishing a forward base from which to attack mainland Japan. This plan would bypass the Philippines, leaving it to its own fate until after the successful conquest and occupation of Japanese islands. The strategy was to let the Japanese forces in South East Asia and the Philippines "wither on the vine."

MacArthur had vowed to return. It was a solemn and binding oath. Nothing less than his personal honor and the honor of his country were at stake. His men, captured at Bataan and Corregidor by the tens of thousands, survivors of the infamous "Death March," were rotting in POW camps like Cabanatuan, Palawan, O'Donnell, and the "Hotel Tacloban." The underground had provided appalling, unspeakable evidence of conditions in the military POW camps. No less oppressive to MacArthur was a sense of brooding guilt associated with the name Santo Tomas. The Filipino guerillas had supplied him with detailed information concerning the internees and their condition. Many of the people at Santo Tomas and Los Banos, its sister camp, were personal friends of the MacArthur's. There were families interned at Santo Tomas whose children he had patted on the head, men whom he had shared politics, business, whiskey and cigars, women whom he had waltzed round the grand ballroom of the Manila Hotel. MacArthur had no doubt that if the Philippines were left to "wither on the vine," all of these lives would wither accordingly. To strike at Formosa would be to seal the fate of ten thousand POWs. He could not compromise. He would not give in. After infuriating, frustrating months of controversy and infighting, he had finally gotten his way. The plans were drawn and implemented. The Philippines would come first.

Task Force Thirty-Eight, the largest naval armada in history, was steaming toward the Philippines under the command of Rear Admirals Montgomery, Bogan, and Sherman. The task force, on the move, covered hundreds of square miles of ocean, stretching from horizon to horizon as far as the eye could see. It was the navy that every commander in history dreamed of.

"I was playing a hopscotch game with my friends one afternoon when we all stopped and looked up at the sky. There was a sound of aircraft engines rapidly building in volume. Suddenly, five silver fighters burst into sight. Flying in a 'V' formation at treetop level, they roared across the campus and were gone before anyone could react in any way. We all froze were we stood. I was counting the seconds, when another fighter, flying alone, banked over the camp on its way to the harbor. This time there could be no mistake. Instead of the familiar Japanese insignia that we used to call the 'fried egg,' the wings of this fighter bore a white star in a field of dark blue, the 'stars and bars' of the U.S. Army Air Forces. He dipped his wings deliberately from side to side, letting us know that the military was aware of us and the nature of the camp."

A crackle of rifle shots followed this lone plane as the Japanese guards recovered from the shock of their surprise, but the fighter was long gone. Far off, the internees could hear the sound of anti-aircraft batteries opening up over downtown Manila.

It took a few seconds for this new, miraculous state of affairs to sink in. Then the camp went wild with joy. People hugged and kissed each other. Straw hats went flying in the air. The joy was short lived, however. Commandant Hayashi was livid with anger. First, even though there had been no air raid warning, not a single guard had gotten a shot off in time. Second, Hayashi was furious with what he considered a disgraceful and insulting conduct of the prisoners during the air raid. They were still under Japanese authority and needed to be reminded of that fact. Their behavior had been most reprehensible.

The commandant ordered the camp to assemble in the main plaza. The entire population was formed in ranks by dorm and room. Hayashi decided a wait in the sun would do them good. Let them remember who they are and where they are. Children cried and begged to sit in the shade. Here and there, a figure would drop out of ranks, fight to maintain balance, then collapse. After an hour or so, Hayashi decided to address them. There would be no further displays like the one he had witnessed that afternoon. When aircraft were sighted, regardless of whether they were Japanese or American, the internees were to avoid looking at them. If the aircraft were close to the camp, internees had the option of crouching by the buildings or hitting the dirt where they were. No waving, signaling, cheering, or shouting of any kind would be permitted in the future. Violators would be punished with the utmost severity. To teach the camp a lesson, he ordered that there be no dinner ration that night.

The camp was still buzzing with excitement in spite of all attempts by the authorities to reassert the status quo. Details of the American airplanes, what type they were, what their mission was likely to be, what kind of armaments they carried, the significance of the wing dips, every conceivable nuance of the brief encounter was discussed repeatedly until the subject was squeezed absolutely dry of information. The rumor mill was working triple time. The Marines have landed in force on Mindanao, Palawan, Negros, Cebu, or Leyte. Japan was on the verge of surrender. Hirohito had been assassinated. For the first time in over three years, there was an air of excitement and expectancy. People who had forgotten how to feel anything but fear and anxiety suddenly remembered the pride and individuality that had been their birthright. By the same token, guards who had been easygoing yesterday were suddenly mean, irritable, and hostile. Regulations that had come to be ignored in the daily routine were now to be enforced to the letter. A new mode of camp survival was forming. To openly show joy or enthusiasm about anything was to invite vicious reprisal.

Internees began to wonder how the Japanese would react when the inevitable invasion came. It was apparent that they were already involved in a life and death race, ready or not. The big question enveloping the collective mind of the camp was, "Will the allies arrive before the Japanese decide to murder us all?"

"The sight of the American planes was thrilling, and watching the happiness of our fellow internees spread through the camp was delightful. There was a new excitement in the air. The order to withhold our dinner that night was tough on us, but the memory of the airplanes gave us comfort and more hope than ever. It eased the hunger pains."

Jean-Marie had a plan, but she held back, keeping it to herself. It had been on her mind for days. Previously, she had thought it too dangerous, but now, new circumstances had given her the courage to seriously consider trying it. There was no use mentioning it to the others. The scheme wouldn't work for more than one person.

An hour after sunset, Jean-Marie was in position, hiding behind a row of garbage cans located to one side of the Japanese pig pens. She was waiting patiently for the guard whose job it was to feed the pigs twice a day. As soon as his back was turned, Jean-Marie was going to rush the pig pen and steal as much of their food as she could possibly carry in the lap of her dress. Then she would run for her life. She thought of the face of her mother, and later Dad and Jimmy, once they saw what she had found to share with them. Wouldn't they be surprised!

"I peeked between the fifty gallon oil drums that the Japanese used as garbage cans. The pigs were agitated. The bigger ones were shoving the weaker ones away from the spot where their food would soon be dumped over the fence. These pigs were not the friendly kind. These pigs were mean as hell. They were mangy, skinny, and constantly hungry. I knew that the boars, given half a chance, would easily take my hand off."

Jean-Marie readied herself for action. It wouldn't be long now. In times gone by, before the military had taken over the camp, there had been a variety of livestock at Santo Tomas. The internees had been allowed to raise chickens, ducks, and hogs. There had even been a cow and two calves. Fresh eggs were better than money, and had become the main means of exchange within the camp. The only item even more sought after was tobacco. Gradually, the animals had sickened and died, killed by the same lack of nutrients that was slowly killing the internees. The Japanese pigs were the only animals still alive within the camp walls, aside from the insects, geckos, and rats.

"I crouched and waited for the guards to arrive. I saw two guards dumping the peelings and scraps of the Japanese kitchen into the pig pen by the fence. They hung around, chatting and smoking and watching the pigs attack the pile of rotting vegetables. I began to get antsy, because the guards were taking their time. If they didn't leave soon, the pigs would finish everything.

"It seemed like forever before the two guards turned and slowly strolled back toward the barracks. I jumped out from behind the oil drums and crawled through the muck to the outskirts of the pigpen, moving as fast as I could on my hands and knees. I crawled to the opposite corner of the pigpen from where the hogs were feeding, leaned over the fence, and made quiet, pig-like noises to try to attract their attention. They ignored me. I pretended to drop something over the fence, and this time they noticed me. The biggest and meanest boar came over to where I stood, followed by the rest of the pigs. As he rooted around in the mud, I quickly ran to the spot where there was a large pile of mushy camotes and wilted greens. In the pile I saw a treasure beyond words: a big heap of fresh potato peels. Mom had told me that potato peels contained more vitamins than the potatoes themselves. I had struck gold! I reached into the pen and began to shovel handfuls of the peels into my lap. Meanwhile, the boar had gotten tired of rooting around and looking for something that wasn't there. He turned around and saw me stealing his dinner. His squeal was earsplitting. Just as I pulled out the last handful of peels, the boar charged at me. I jumped up, with my dress folded and holding the potato peels, and turned and ran straight into the legs of a Japanese guard. I bounced back with the recoil and landed on my butt. The guard looked down, scowling, hands on his hips, leaning forward, looming over me. Suddenly he burst into a belly laugh. I sprang to my feet, with my eyes glued on the guard. He took a big step towards me, made a ferocious face and grunted, 'HUUHHH!' and scared the living daylights out of me. I turned and ran so fast, my feet hardly touched the ground.

"Once I got the few potato peelings I was able to hang on to back to the Annex, I showed them to my mother. I never told her about the guard. Mom and I waited until the middle of the night to eat them. When it seemed like everyone in the Annex room was finally asleep, we tried to chew and swallow as quietly as we could. We knew what it was like to hear someone eating, while you tossed on your cot with your insides crying out with the pain of hunger."

Jean-Marie and her mother ate in total silence, both of them savoring the flavor of the potato peels and the sensation of the food between their teeth. The potato peels acted immediately on the horrible gnawing sensation and relentless demands of their hunger. For the rest of that long night, Jean-Marie and her mother would sleep blissfully silent and still.

Although most of the work assignments for internees were within the walls of Santo Tomas, there were rare occasions where a work assignment would take internees beyond the camp walls and into the city. The wood collection detail was one of these assignments. There were typically about fifteen men on a wood detail, each with a red armband identifying him as a POW laborer. The men were expected to fill three big caramatas daily and haul them back to the camp kitchen. They were guarded by an escort of four Japanese soldiers, although the guards were hardly necessary. Most of the men had families still in the camp.

Because the chopping and hauling was the most demanding physical work of any to be done at Santo Tomas, the men of the wood detail were allowed extra rations. They got a third more than the rest of the camp, bringing their total to over a thousand grams a day. In addition, the wood and garbage details were the main channels for black market smuggling. The Japanese guards and the internees working on these details had an unspoken understanding concerning the laws of supply and demand. As long as the guards got what they considered to be a fair slice of the action, all sorts of goods could be obtained, including tobacco, needles, thread, cloth, and anything small enough to stuff into a pair of shorts. News of conditions in Manila was another precious item that could only be supplied by the wood and garbage crews. Many of those confined behind the walls had Filipino husbands, wives, and children who, not being enemy aliens in the eyes of the authorities, had not been interned. Sporadic smuggled messages were the only way they could hear any news of each other.

"Dad was assigned to one of these wood details, and was actually pretty happy about it. Even though the work was harder than most in the camp, he was able to go outside the camp for awhile. Dad told us later that when he took his first unobstructed look down the Calle Espana, it was a surreal experience for him. The broad, peaceful street looked almost exactly as it had when we had lived on Del Pilar.

"He and his work crew labored all day in the ruins of a catholic church, taking out the usable firewood from the mounds of bombed out rubble. Dad said it was strange work knowing that the kitchen fires back in camp would be fueled with crushed pews and prayer stools, splintered confessionals, and fragments of holy images.

All along the route back to Santo Tomas, behind the backs of the Japanese guards, people gave them hidden victory signs, smiles, and nods of encouragement. The overwhelming majority of the Filipinos were pro-American. Many were involved in the underground. The Japanese had fallen into the classic position of the hated conqueror/foreign occupier. During the day, the cities and military strong points were under Japanese control. During the night, a Japanese soldier was safest in the company of large groups of his comrades or behind the walls of a fortified compound. Night or day, almost the entire rural countryside of the Philippine Islands belonged to the guerillas.

About a mile from the camp, the progress of the wood detail was halted by the presence of a large crowd of Filipinos. The press of staring, silent people completely blocked off the intersection. One of the guards made his way through the mob to find out what has blocking the street. Both guards and internees were anxious to get back to camp. The afternoon thunder clouds were brewing overhead and the air was thick with humidity, making it hard to bear the snail's pace of the big carts. After a few minutes, a small detachment of Japanese military police arrived at a trot, shoving with rifle butts and poking with fixed bayonets, clearing a path through the crowd so that the wood detail could continue. Gene noticed that the Japanese soldiers were unusually nervous, poised for action. He wondered what was up. The two hundred or so assembled Filipinos were silent and grim, and some were weeping. Tension crackled, and it seemed that in spite of the guns and bayonets, at any moment the crowd might rush the Japanese and overwhelm them.

Gene pulled his cart through the lane formed by the soldiers and reached the intersection. There he saw a small horse drawn carriage, surrounded by soldiers with their guns leveled on the mass of faces around them. Several Japanese officers, holding pistols in their hands, were overseeing the situation. The troops waited for orders to fire.

Stretched out on the road behind the cart were the naked, mangled bodies of three people, with their hands still tied to the axle of the cart. Gene could see that one of the corpses had been a woman, but the rest were too maimed to easily guess their sex. They had been dragged behind the cart until almost all of the skin on their bodies had been torn off. Their black hair hung down in bloody clumps over the horror masks that had been their faces. As Gene pulled his cart by this grisly scene, he looked into the back seat of the death carriage and suddenly realized what he was seeing, why the Filipinos seemed so near to open revolt, and why the Japanese seemed so ill at ease.

Lying on the back seat were the torn habits of three nuns.

"Dad couldn't believe it. Those were nuns dangling from the rear axle. It seemed impossible. All the way back to the main gate, he struggled to comprehend what he had seen. When he finally got back, he was as pale as a ghost and he looked older than I'd ever seen him. He was talking with my mother at a distance from me, and I don't think he meant for me to hear what he said next. In a hushed voice, he looked at my mother and said, 'Jesus God, Eileen! If they'd do that to *nuns*, what are they going to do to us?' I quickly turned away and pretended that I didn't hear him.

"That night when I went to bed, I had a nightmare of several Japanese guards leading my mother and me out the front gate to the Calle Espana. Lieutenant Abiko was there, with a rope in his hands, standing in front of a wooden cart, smiling at us. I woke up in a cold sweat."

Jean-Marie was playing pick-up-sticks one morning with her two friends, Jean and Bonnie, when they heard the Japanese gun batteries starting up again. This wasn't entirely unexpected, since the downtown defenses had started popping their anti-aircraft guns off at five that morning and had continued at random times since then. It was already an hour after breakfast. The girls looked up and saw what appeared to be another mock dogfight that the Japanese fighter pilots would engage in from time to time. Three fighters were practicing dodging and weaving in dogfight patterns.

"We had seen this before, but never so close to the camp. The fighters were maybe a quarter of a mile away. Suddenly, one of the planes burst into flames and began to disintegrate. It passed out of sight over the rooftops on the other side of the main gate. Moments later, there was a muffled explosion and a huge flame with black smoke shot into the air. I was shocked. Before I had a chance to figure out what happened to the Japanese fighter, I could hear a roar of aircraft engines growing. It sounded different than before. Not with the mean snarl of fighters, or with the high whine of dive bombers. Instead, it was a deep, steady, reverberating tone. It sounded like an organ, growing deeper and louder by the second."

In another second, a wedge formation of twenty, low flying bombers cruised over the camp at about two thousand feet. Internees were pointing and shouting as the first wave of aircraft was followed by another and another. The big planes were a thrilling sight, with sunlight bouncing in glaring bursts off their silver surfaces, their wings colorful with U.S.A.A.F. decals, their fuselages bristling with machine guns, cannons, and radio antennae. Higher up in the sky another formation of bombers became visible, literally dozens of bombers, flying in triangular wedges of three planes each. Then, all too soon, they were gone in the direction of the harbor.

"I ran to tell my parents what we had seen, running through a campus filled with people milling about, laughing and dancing with joy or sobbing in an overflow of emotion. Japanese soldiers were running through the crowd in complete confusion, shouting random orders at each other while scrambling for their battle stations. Somewhere, an air raid siren began to wail the 'all clear.' I couldn't find Mom or Dad in all the excitement, and I lost sight of Bonnie, Jean, and my brother, Jimmy. I stopped running in front of the Education Building, gasping and out of breath, letting the pandemonium break around me. I saw other internees running past me, seeking their families or shelter. At the same time, I looked up towards the roof of the Education Building and saw a crew of Japanese machine gunners. I saw one of the officers standing to one side, scanning the harbor area with his binoculars."

From the direction of the harbor came the steady pounding of the anti-aircraft batteries and the continual hammering of machine guns, mixed with the scream of falling bombs. A moment later, hundreds of shattering, overlapping explosions could be heard, as the bomb patterns hit the ground.

"I was standing in the Main Building, looking past the open doors, and saw the air outside was getting dark and hazy. It was a very creepy and scary feeling. Suddenly, all I wanted was to be with Mom, Dad, and Jimmy."

It was 10:30 a.m. on Thursday, September 21, 1944.

The first U.S. air strikes against the Japanese in Manila had begun.

Three more times that day, major air attacks were mounted on harbor and oil storage depots and on the city's airfields. A murky, acrid pall lay over Manila, fed by raging flames and billowing plumes of reeking black smoke.

The pilots of the American planes kept perfect formation, coming in on a beam that ignored the Japanese defenses. Rank after rank dived low through the flak cover, obliterating their targets and banking off to strive for higher altitudes. With each wave of bombing and strafing, there were less anti-aircraft guns left to challenge the Americans. The heavy B-17 Flying Fortress and B-24 Liberator bombers were accompanied by swarms of fighters -- P-51 Mustangs, P-61 Black Widows, and F6F Grumman Wildcats -- that seemed to have emptied the sky of Japanese aircraft in the first few minutes of fighting. Off on the horizon, the sprawling industrial zone of the Pandacan oil district was under massive air attack. Now and then, huge storage tanks would burst with a tremendous roar. The colossal explosions would send shock waves over the rooftops of Manila. Torpedo bombers caught a large black Japanese supply freighter steaming out of the harbor. It suddenly disappeared in a vast, bursting column of flame, steam, and rocketing debris. Moments later, the only trace of the freighter that remained was a huge and perfect smoke ring, a half mile wide, that hovered over the water for a few minutes until the breeze eventually blew it away.

The air over Santo Tomas began to rain a thick, sooty ash. Tiny fragments of glowing debris were floating down to smolder on the wet ground.

Fires were breaking out all over the city. The air raid was over by late afternoon, and by curfew that night, the internees of Santo Tomas were exhausted, but exhilarated. Jean-Marie was too excited to go to sleep. She wasn't alone in her agitation. Hardly anyone in the camp felt like sleeping. Suddenly, life was just too full of promise.

"I hopped out of my cot and walked over to the bathroom tap to get a drink of water. I put my head in the sink, mouth under the tap, and turned the faucet. I pulled my head out of the sink so fast I almost broke my neck. Instead of the lukewarm stream of water I was used to, a bunch of brown mud burst from the pipe and covered my mouth and chin. I backed off a step and wiped the slime from my face. The faucet was going berserk. There was air and mud sputtering out of the faucet, but no water. The wall pipes were loudly groaning in a way I'd never heard before. I was afraid to turn off the faucet... the sink seemed like it was getting ready to self-destruct.

"Suddenly, my mother came into the bathroom and turned off the faucet. It took her a few moments to realize what was happening. The thought of being without water scared her deeply. I immediately thought of the toilets, and what they'd be like after an hour without reliable running water. There was the laundry and the showers, too. But most of all, we needed water to drink. Well, as it turned out, we didn't have to worry. The Japanese had apparently turned off the water earlier that day during the air raids."

That night, as Jean-Marie curled up in her cot and fell asleep, she entered a dream that made the corners of her mouth stretch into a smile. Even in her dream state, she recognized that she had dreamt this before. And she was glad to be back.

She was in her grandmother's ice cream store in that faraway place called California, savoring every scoop of ice cream that she could spoon into her mouth.

Jean-Marie was playing dolls with her friends one afternoon, when Eileen found her and told her to follow her. Apparently, the Japanese wanted all of the internees at the Education Building for reasons unknown. With the recent convolution wrought by the bombings and the American forces evidently getting closer to the point of invasion, rumors had been flowing fast and furious concerning an evacuation, followed by a death march to some far off location in the mountains. To Eileen, these rumors had a ring of truth. Los Banos Internment Camp had been populated with almost two thousand internee "volunteers" from Santo Tomas. Eileen dreaded this sudden call for the camp to assemble. She was sure they'd be told to gather their possessions and make ready to move out.

Jean-Marie and her mother joined the mob of internees waiting outside the entrance to the Education Building and, after a few minutes, located Gene and Jimmy. Under the eyes of the bored guards, they speculated on what was happening.

Family groups were sorted out of the mob and moved into the building. Single internees without relatives in the camp were counted off in groups of five and taken inside. This went on for over an hour before one of the supply officers called the name "Faggiano" from the lobby.

Gene, Eileen, Jean-Marie, and Jimmy were led to the administration office. The officer told them to take a seat and wait. Sitting in chairs was a novelty for the children, because chairs were a rare item in the camp. Some internees had actually gone into business making chairs out of scrap wood, but the furniture generally didn't last more than a month or two. Adults came to associate the act of sitting in a chair, instead of on a cot or a mat of sawali, as a symbol of the pre-war good life.

"Mom and Dad were worried, and Jimmy and I could see it. Not knowing what was taking place left them feeling helpless. They exchanged their theories in low undertones, until they ran out of conjecture and speculation. Dad took in our situation and decided to teach Jimmy and me a new song. It got a laugh out of Mom, and managed to keep her mind off of morbid fantasies."

When the officer finally came back, he wasn't alone. With him was a Japanese lieutenant who seemed too young to be an officer. The young lieutenant bowed and introduced himself in perfect English, with no trace of an accent. He handed Gene and Eileen a multi-page form with two pencils, and politely informed them that they were required to fill out all information in detail, requesting extra paper as needed. The lieutenant claimed that a census of all POWs was underway.

"As soon as he left the room, Mom and Dad began to worry again. Neither one believed the lieutenant's story about a census. They had filled out identical forms on numerous occasions, and scanning the pages they found that, as always, the main focus of the questions concerned their assets, how much money was stored in what bank, what names the accounts were held under, what properties were owned, who held the deed, and so forth. No internee in his right mind would dream of giving the authorities accurate financial information. Those naive few who had were later informed that their holdings had been converted into Japanese currency."

Gene and Eileen tried desperately to remember what they had written on the last forms the Japanese had given to them months ago. The form also had questions dealing with the skills and job titles held by the internees in civilian life. This was a new question, and a dangerous line of inquiry. Through the underground telegraph, the internees of Santo Tomas had been aware of major events in Cabanatuan, the largest of the nearby military camps. The POWs there had been required to list their skills only days before entire convoys of the prisoners had been sent to heavy labor camps in Japan, Formosa, Manchuria, and the Philippines.

Gene listed his occupation as "clerk," Eileen as "housewife." Under assets, they wrote "none." On the second sheet of paper were questions the likes of which they had never seen before on a Japanese form.

"Do you believe the war could have been avoided?"

"Do you believe in war?"

"Have the Filipinos been kind to you?"

"Give one instance of how they were kind to you and who they were. How do you know they were sincerely kind to you?"

To these loaded questions, Gene and Eileen gave the vaguest possible answers.

When the young lieutenant returned, he collected the forms and directed them to another office. There, another young officer they had never seen before was adjusting the focus on a huge, antique camera. He didn't speak English, but using sign language, he instructed the family, much to their astonishment, to arrange themselves for a group portrait. When the officer looked through the viewfinder and ascertained that they were in the proper positions, he walked up to them and pinned a piece of cardboard to Gene's ragged t-shirt. A long series of numbers were printed in heavy black characters across the face of the cardboard. Powder flashed in the pan and the number was removed.

Inmates of German death camps were only too familiar with this procedure, and others like it, but as the Faggiano's were led to the rear exit and back out to the campus, they could not begin to understand what had just taken place.

It had been two days since the last bombing, and life at the camp was returning to normal. The absence of American planes could be interpreted in a variety of ways, and all possible variations had developed a following of true believers. The Americans had decided that the Philippines were too heavily defended, and had decided not to attack. The Americans had merely been testing the Japanese defenses, and would land at any moment in overwhelming force. The Americans had been beaten in a huge sea battle off the coast of Palawan. The Japanese had attempted an invasion of Australia, and American forces were fully occupied in defending the Aussie front. The Americans had already landed in force, and huge land battles were raging all over the islands. The only thing that was certain was that the Japanese guards and officers were more relaxed with each day that an air raid failed to take place, and the internees became more depressed and anxious. Where were the American planes? What was happening in the outside world?

Jean-Marie had spent the entire afternoon unsuccessfully begging from the new batch of Japanese soldiers. They were by far the stingiest bunch she had yet to encounter. She had used up all her cutest ploys, her cleverest phrases of Japanese, without earning the smallest return for her efforts. Getting angry meant getting feisty, and Jean-Marie decided she wasn't about to give up until she had tested every last one of them. By then, it would be time for dinner.

The new troops had arrived at dawn, piled out of the four heavy trucks that had brought them, and immediately proceeded to set up a tent city, covering most of the campus area that had not already been turned into vegetable gardens. With the soldiers came truckloads of military supplies. Locked rooms -- where dozens of suitcases and packages that were brought into the camp by the prisoners at the beginning of the war and confiscated by orders of the military police -- were suddenly thrown open, with the contents emptied in a heap on the road. A mob of internees combed through the pile, searching for lost possessions. Occasional fights broke out as ownership of one item or another was claimed by several people at once. An hour later, nothing was left but a sad, crushed heap of empty boxes. Squads of Japanese troops filled the newly created space with ammunition and canned rations.

As it turned out, there were far more soldiers -- over two hundred -- than tents. The camp was thrown into turmoil as many internees were forced to give up their living space for the newly arrived troops.

Over a hundred internees found themselves faced with the prospect of taking up permanent residence in the halls of the main buildings. After much debate, a delegation composed of several of the more influential internees marched to the commandant's office with the purpose of filing a formal protest. It was against the terms of the Geneva Convention to store war materials in a POW camp. They were reminded, for the hundredth time, that the Japanese government had never approved the Geneva Convention, and they were assured, for the hundredth time, that their concerns would be viewed with the most serious consideration.

All day long, military supplies continued to pour into the camp. Crowds were beginning to move toward the kitchen line area. Dinner was an hour away.

"I was about to join the others in line when I heard the sound of a commotion growing in the vicinity of the guard's kitchen bodega. I trotted over to the area where the noise was coming from to find out what was causing the ruckus. At the center of attention were two of the newly arrived Japanese soldiers. One was holding two small Filipino water buffaloes, called carabao, by a lead rope, while the other was trying in vain to communicate with the prisoners. He was finally able to explain to them that he and his friend had a deal to make. If the internees would agree to butcher and quarter the two animals, they would be repaid with a portion of the meat. Immediately, dozens of internees volunteered for the job.

"The first problem the volunteers had was the lack of tools with which to slaughter the animals. One of the soldiers left for a few minutes and returned with three bayonets. When he returned, he was accompanied by several more new soldiers, all of whom were grinning as if they shared some hilarious, private joke among themselves."

The bayonets were distributed to the internees, and the butchering began. They tied the animals to a fence post and slit their throats, and the creatures were hardly dead before the internees began to skin them. More soldiers came over and brought an empty cart. They lit cigarettes and chatted among themselves, as the internees worked to cut the carcasses apart.

Finally the job was done. None of the internees had had the strength to work from beginning to end, so they had taken turns, each one keeping tabs on how many ways the meat would have to be divided. This was quite a sight for Jean-Marie, as a dozen men and women were soon dark red with bloodstains and gore up to their elbows. The soldiers insisted that the butchers clean the bayonets before they were returned. Then the guards bowed with mock politeness to the waiting crowd and thanked them for their labor.

"It didn't take long for us to figure out why they were smiling the way they did at the beginning of the slaughter. The guards said 'domo arigato' to us, and then proceeded to heave the heavy chunks of bloody meat into the cart. Meanwhile, we kept waiting for the moment when we would receive our share. Slowly, it dawned on us that the guards weren't going to leave anybody any of the meat from either carabao. We watched the Japanese load the cart until nothing was left on the ground but the hides and the guts, lying in a pool of coagulating blood and swarming with flies."

Without a backwards glance, the soldiers hauled the cart toward the guard's kitchen. The silent crowd began to realize that the only meat they were going to see was lying on the ground at their feet. A mad race for the remaining scraps broke out. Men and women fought furiously for a piece of intestine, or for shreds of meat clinging to the hooves or the tail. All sense of shame or civilized consideration was lost in the scramble.

"In the midst of the frenzy, I ended up claiming one piece of the carabao hide by standing on it and refusing to get off of it. No matter how hard I was shoved or kicked, I refused to budge. In a matter of minutes, the piece of carabao hide that I had claimed became an island under my feet, as the rest was hacked away and torn into fragments. The instant the last piece was cut free from my little island of flesh, I quickly grabbed the piece of hide in a two-handed death grip and sprinted for the Annex.

"When I caught up with Mom and Dad, I showed them my trophy. I had a whole square foot of stinking hide in my hands. Dad decided to try frying the piece of hide. He opened the cloth bag he wore around his neck and removed his most precious possession: an old, worn, Gillette razor blade. The double-edged safety razor had been sharpened and resharpened over the last two years, until it had been reduced to half its original size. The Gillette Company would have been gratified to learn all the thousands of uses my father had found for their product. It had given haircuts to many of the men and boys living in the Gym, it had been used to cut clothes, splice palm fibers for sawali matting, drain infections, and slice sandal soles out of rubber tires."

Gene proceeded to use the blade for what was, no doubt, a Gillette first: scraping the bristles off a raw carabao hide. After the prospective meal was made as hairless as could be hoped for, the whole family made a visit to Shantytown, searching for a hut with a charcoal cooking pot in working order. After some haggling, they came to an arrangement with a fellow internee. In exchange for a strip of hide one inch wide and about a foot and a half long, they could use his cooking facilities.

"We could not have possibly imagined how tough the skin of a carabao would prove to be. Mom poured a small pool of cod liver oil in the black frying pan. She had saved a supply from the last Red Cross packages months ago, and had been forcing me to swallow a half a teaspoonful a day. The Red Cross supply of cold cream was long gone, and cod liver oil was all she had left to cook with. As the hide fried, it began to curl up into a tight ball, shriveling in upon itself. Dad flipped it over in the pan, hoping it would flatten out under its own weight, but instead it began to curl up the other way.

"Dad gave up trying to fry the hide, and instead decided to try and boil it. Boiling makes hard things soft, so he figured sooner or later the hide would soften and act the way normal food does. He brought the water to a boil, dumped the hide in and left it there to cook for almost an hour. After an hour, he lifted the hide out of the pot and proceeded to cut it into thin strips, kind of like beef jerky. He then cut the strips so that each separate piece was a square about two inches on a side. We each put a piece in our mouth and began to chew. And chew. And chew. It seemed like the longer we chewed, the bigger the piece got! My piece got so big, in fact, that it eventually filled my entire mouth. We gave up and spit the chunks of hide out. Dad was getting mad, but he wasn't beaten yet. He cut each of the pieces in half, and then in half again, and told us to put it in our mouths. He said, 'All right! Don't try and chew it. At the count of three, just swallow! Get ready. One... two... three... swallow!' That did it. As long as the piece was small enough, and as long as we didn't chew, we could get it down. A half hour later, the carabao hide was gone, sitting like a pile of bricks in our stomachs."

"Dougout Doug" had been a nickname that many internees had for General Douglas MacArthur. People had started calling him that when he left the doomed defenders of Bataan for the island fortress of Corregidor. Bataan held out against overwhelming odds for fourteen weeks. Lieutenant General Masaharu Homma, conqueror of the Philippines, was under immense pressure from his superiors in Tokyo to wipe out the last pocket of enemy resistance. Finally, cut off on the tip of the Bataan peninsula at Mariveles and surrounded by fresh Japanese reinforcements, Major General Edward King, Jr. had been forced to surrender on April 9, 1942, months after the rest of the Philippines had been overrun. Seventy-five thousand men would make the infamous "Death March" sixty miles north to Camp O'Donnell. At least one out of every ten men would die on the way.

A month after the fall of Bataan, after enduring weeks of saturation bombardment, the 11,000 men of Corregidor Island surrendered. Most of them were literally down to their last bullet and last can of rations. The already starved survivors of Corregidor were jammed into the hold of a Japanese freighter, where they spent a week with no food or water. They were then marched through the streets of Manila, where the Filipinos were encouraged to throw garbage at their former "white colonial masters." Most had ended up interned at Cabanatuan.

Internees at Santo Tomas had spent the first three months of their captivity filled with hope, watching the Bataan battle glow in the night sky and listening all day to the dull thunder of distant artillery. Gradually, the red glow faded, and then the roaring of the huge mortars of Corregidor died away and were not heard again. Even after seeing the photos of the

American generals surrendering, photos of thousands of their men with their hands in the air, many refused to believe that Bataan had fallen. The expected short stay at Santo Tomas had turned into three long years. MacArthur had left Corregidor two weeks before the surrender, smuggled out aboard torpedo boat PT-41. From Mindanao, the MacArthur's had been flown to Australia.

Many internees, including Gene, didn't resent MacArthur for saving himself and his family. It made sense that such an important American military man shouldn't fall into enemy hands. The thing that got their goat was that they heard he had smuggled out most of his household staff -- a cook, a maid, a chauffeur, and an amah -- to accompany him to his new headquarters.

For many of the internees, until MacArthur came striding through the gates of Santo Tomas, "Dougout Doug" he would remain.

Chapter Five

October 1944

Jean-Marie and Jimmy had a plan. One day they noticed a drainage ditch with a long rainwater runoff pipe that went into a low, moss and weed covered dirt embankment and out under the wall. In their child minds, this was their ticket out, their own private door to the outside world. The corroded, red and orange rusted length of pipe was far too narrow for an adult to wriggle into, but they knew that they could do it if they had to. The guards never watched them in a serious way, it seemed, and they guessed they could, with any luck, sprint across the grounds and be up into the pipe without being noticed. Jean-Marie knew instinctively that being small and grubby helped, because they tended to blend into the landscape. Adults normally didn't notice them.

"The big question was, once we got in the pipe, then what? In the dry season we had seen huge spiders, long snakes, and mangy rats crawl from the pipe and race across the open ground. The rats were the biggest danger. They had razor sharp teeth and wouldn't hesitate to attack a helpless human being, especially one our size. In the wet season, the drainpipe was full of muddy rainwater. If the rains had been mild for a few days, there might be perhaps a few inches of empty space at the topmost curve of the pipe. But how far did the pipe go beyond the wall? We had no idea. And how far would we have to crawl before we found a way out, if there even was a way out? There was no way of knowing for certain."

Jean-Marie had spent long, hungry nights considering all the possibilities of the journey through the drainpipe. She saw herself and her brother crawling blindly, deep in the ground, under the silent, nighttime streets. Sometimes, in her visions, she and Jimmy would emerge safe and free in another drainage ditch just across the Calle Forbes. On other nights she would imagine them struggling forward on shredded elbows and knees, lost and exhausted, caught for eternity in a nightmare maze of endless, branching tunnels until they drowned in the sewage or were torn apart by leaping rats. Her biggest fear, though, was coming out of the tunnel and being met by a group of Japanese guards, ready to run them through with their bayonets.

"Jimmy and I decided to use the drainpipe only if Mom and Dad were killed. That was the deciding factor. Only at that point, and not until that point, would it be worth it to take the risk. Meanwhile, when Jimmy and I were particularly frightened, when things in the camp took a turn for the worse, we could visit the drainpipe and reassure ourselves that it was still there."

One afternoon, the guards had marched through the camp to hang a new large signboard near the main gate, facing the Calle Espana. The board contained yet another new set of endless "ukase," military edicts, for the behavior of the Filipino residents of Manila.

"As soon as we read what was on the board, we just shook our heads. No wonder the Filipinos hated the Japanese so much. There had been so many of these kinds of proclamations in the past few months, you would've had to be a genius in order to memorize and act in compliance with them all."

The sign read:

Notice

1. Salute to the Japanese soldiers when you meet them.

2. The Japanese flag should be displayed at every house's door.

3. Everybody must put the sunrise armband on the left arm.

4. Everybody should have the certificate of residence.

5. The Japanese soldier is your good friend. Whenever you see Japanese soldiers you must welcome them and not escape from them. The escaper will be considered as the enemy.

6. Unless you do not tell false price you will be payed reasonably.

7. You are absolutely prohibited to walk from sunset to sunrise without carrying lamps. The walker who had not lights will be shot by the Japanese patrolling soldier without any warns.

8. The holding of arms is allowed by the army but the holder should report to the mayor and get permission from Japanese authority.

9. The incendiaries accidental fire and robbery will be punished by dead.

10. Don't be fooled and bewildered by false propaganda spread by communists and Chinese.

11. The jobless people can find one's job with the Japanese army and with the Japanese authorities.

12. Be OBDIENT to the orders of Governor and Mayor who are authorized by Imperial Japanese army.

By order of the Commandant
Lt. Col. T. Hayashi
Imperial Army of Japan

"We laughed at the obvious misspellings and bad grammar, especially being 'OBDIENT' to the orders of the Governor and Mayor. The sign actually provided a bit of lightheartedness for the group of internees I was standing around. One man said, 'Yeah, the Japanese soldier is your friend all right... and with friends like that, who in the hell needs enemies?'"

Gene and Eileen didn't have much to give their daughter on her ninth birthday. It had been the same way for Jimmy in January. Before the war broke out, birthday celebrations were a big event in the Faggiano household. There would be cake, ice cream, balloons, singing, and of course, lots of presents. Since their internment, however, the party had shrunk considerably. Gone were the balloons, ice cream, and cake. Gene and Eileen would still sing, though, and they fashioned presents for the children with whatever material they had on hand at the time. Eileen would usually knit something for the kids, and Gene would whittle a doll or a toy soldier from a piece of wood. Jimmy and Jean-Marie did the best they could for their parents, too, even if it was just a huge hug and a kiss.

"I got the shock of my life when this boy in the camp, that I had a crush on, walked up to me and wished me a happy birthday. I was surprised that he even knew when my birthday was! It turned out that he asked my brother and Jimmy told him October fifteenth. Well, the boy smiled at me and then handed me a gift. I couldn't believe how shy and embarrassed I got! He gave me a lens from a pair of broken sunglasses, and a piece of leather strap that he'd found. He then proceeded to instruct me on how to use the two together. He said, 'First, put the leather strap around your head so that it covers one of your eyes. Then, hold the sunglass lens up to the other eye! It's like you have a real pair of sunglasses on!'

"You'd be surprised how little things like that can mean so much."

One morning, Jean-Marie, Jimmy, and Gene were sitting together at a wooden table with a group of other internees, and having their usual breakfast of lugao and coconut milk. Jean-Marie was relating a story she had heard from her friend Bonnie, and was doing more talking than eating. Towards the end of her conversation, Gene and Jimmy had almost finished the small portions they each had on their plates, while Jean-Marie's food was still relatively untouched.

"Dad finally stood up to head off to his work assignment, and as soon as he did, this teenage boy leaned over my plate and spit right into my food. I was shocked, as was everyone at the table. Then the teenager, acting as if his spit had served to stake a claim on it, reached out for my breakfast. I beat him to it, quickly wrapping my hands around the edges of the plate. The kid was twice my size, but he wasn't going to get my food without a fight.

"I had grown so self-reliant that I had totally forgotten the presence of my father and brother. I didn't expect any help from the outside world. Suddenly, a fist came from nowhere and sent the teenage boy flying. The boy sprang to his feet, but Dad decked him again with a blow to the side of his head. I was crouching over, protecting my food. The boy was getting up for the second time, and Dad was waiting. I had never seen my father in a rage like this. The next thing you know, the teenager's father got involved and was now fighting Dad, too. This is when Jimmy jumped into the fray.

While Dad fought the father of the teenager, Jimmy was fighting the kid. It was a complete brawl."

The rest of the breakfasters had rapidly retired from the table, keeping their mugs and trays well away from the action. Some hung around to cheer the combatants on. Others walked away in disgust, feeling more like the inmates of a zoo than a human community. A flash of red armbands showed up as the internee police arrived on the scene. In no time the brawl was over. The camp cops separated the bleeding, gasping men with a time-tested, professional mixture of force, threats, and appeals to higher reason.

The team leader of the internee patrol had reached the end of his patience. Breakfast wasn't over yet and already there had been three fights, one after another. He squared off in front of Gene, Jimmy, the teenager, and his father, and scolded them for their behavior. Gene interjected, "Just tell this guy that if his kid ever spits into my daughter's food again, I'll kill the sonofabitch!" The internee patrol leader gave Gene a quick look in the eye that conveyed to Gene, in a split second, that he understood the reason for his anger, but he couldn't take sides. Then, as quickly, he said to the group, "All right, enough already, I understand plenty. But you need to understand that it won't be long now, gentlemen, and we need to keep our spirits up! Let's not do the job of the Japs for them, ok?"

As the team leader and his men walked away, Gene turned to his daughter, expecting her to be distraught. He was about to comfort her for the loss of her food and promise to make it up to her, when he saw her sitting at the table, looking up at her father and holding a now empty plate.

While the men had been talking, Jean-Marie had finished her breakfast to the last grain.

"It seemed that many of us were beginning to fear Commandant Hayashi's right-hand man, Lieutenant Abiko, more and more. His brutal behavior reflected his personal hatred of us, and it seemed to grow by the day. Personally, I think that he saw us as cowards, weak and pitiful. He was the archetype of what we referred to as the 'bad Jap.' I knew that he could be capable of cruelty. The incident in the Annex with my mother was still etched in my brain. But nothing shocked me more than when my father told us about what Abiko did to Bumblebee.

"According to Dad, he heard that Bumblebee had done something that got the attention of the Japanese guards made them angry. Dad didn't know if he stole some food from the Japanese bodega or what, but whatever he did, Lieutenant Abiko decided to make an example out of him. Bumblebee was struck repeatedly by the guards with the butts of their rifles. Once he was lying on the ground, two guards forced a large tin funnel past his lips and down his throat. They held it in place, while a third guard emptied gallon after gallon of water down the funnel. Bumblebee had to swallow it or drown. Just before he reached the point when he would begin to vomit the water back up, two guards reached down and wrapped their hands around his jaw, while four more guards held his arms and legs, keeping him on his back. Then, while the guards held him in place, Abiko stomped on Bumblebee's stomach.

Jean-Marie was never able to confirm what she heard was true, but knowing Abiko and his hatred of the prisoners, it didn't seem far out of the realm of possibility.

"Knowing Bumblebee, if this story was true he probably wouldn't talk about it. I saw him near the Education Building not long after my dad told me what he heard, and Bumblebee was playing catch with some children, laughing and having a good old time. He saw me and waved, smiling that smile of his. I thought that if what I heard was true, and Abiko's goal was to break this man's spirit, then he failed miserably."

Regardless of whether what Gene heard about Bumblebee was true or not, one thing was for certain: the punishment rate of internees, even for the smallest infractions, was on the rise and was getting more severe.

Chapter Six

November 1944

"BETTER LEYTE THAN NEVER"

Rumors began to circulate. The improbable became the possible, and the possible became the actual. On October 20, 1944, the U.S. Sixth Army had invaded the Philippines.

MacArthur was back.

Some people spent all day losing themselves in their work assignments, some in dreaming about food. Confirmed smokers demolished hours of stagnant time outside the guard barracks and troop tents, scouring the ground, inch by inch, for cigarette butts. Others cheated tedious hours and minutes by availing themselves of the continual round of marathon card games.

Month after month, the American advance crept over the vast expanse of the Pacific with an agonizing lack of speed, quarter-inching toward the Philippines. After years of this waiting game, knowing that American troops in unknown numbers had actually landed and watching Manila getting wasted by daily air raids, the entire internee population was coming down with a bad case of "invasion fever." People were beginning to take chances. Arrests for petty or serious offenses were increasing every day. The Japanese, more impulsive and unpredictable than ever, had arrested an elderly man for possession of an unauthorized plate of beans. They had sentenced a woman to three weeks in the guard house for stealing a papaya from the garden. Internees were running out of patience. No one seemed to have the endurance to put up with "ukase" anymore. The internee/Japanese relationship was deteriorating as the internees grew more confident, and the guards became more anxious and depressed.

Rumor after rumor made the rounds, most of them sounding too good to be true. Gradually, smuggled messages from the underground confirmed even the most optimistic reports. The Americans had established a solid beachhead on Leyte and were steadily pushing back the Japanese Thirty-Fifth Army, commanded by General Suzuki. A vast sea battle, perhaps the largest in history, had been fought in the Leyte Gulf. After three days of

71

ferocious fighting, the Japanese navy had been devastated, losing four aircraft carriers, three battleships, eight cruisers, twelve destroyers, and more than ten thousand sailors and marines. The islands were completely cut off, blockaded by the victorious American ships. General MacArthur made a dramatic entrance through the surf and announced, "People of the Philippines, I have returned! By the grace of Almighty God, our forces stand again on Philippine soil."

A quarter million Japanese soldiers in the Philippines could expect nothing by way of reinforcements or supplies. Bombing raids over Manila were taking place at the rate of two or three a day, and it was evident to all that the city would eventually be taken. Defending anti-aircraft fire was becoming more and more pointless, as American dive bombers and fighters destroyed gun positions and annihilated their crews. Japanese aircraft had practically disappeared from the skies. In desperation, the first use of a kamikaze aircraft took place following the Leyte landings, when a kamikaze plane hit an Australian heavy cruiser on October 21st.

Flights of P-38 Lightning fighters bombed and strafed Japanese positions at will. Strongholds, such as the main post office, Manila City Hall, or the church of San Sebastian, became isolated fortresses amidst spreading fields of rubble. During the first weeks of the war, the Allies had realized that Manila was indefensible. They had retired to the natural fortresses of Bataan and Corregidor, declaring Manila an "open city." Perhaps the Japanese would shortly do the same.

Slowly, reluctantly, the internees of the Santo Tomas Internment Camp began to come down from a week of intense emotion. Life had to be lived. The "boys" were still hundreds of miles away, with a vast, suicidal Japanese army dug in between them and Manila.

Jean-Marie and Eileen were working on the rice cleaning detail, known in the Santo Tomas Internment Camp as the A.B.C. girls. Twenty bony women, wearing faded cotton prints, worn khaki shorts, wide, ragged, straw hats, or bleached bandanas over their hair, worked at a long wooden table in the shade of the Annex building, feet resting on the cool, wet ground. Sporadic air raids had been taking place all day, but the action was far to the north over Clark Field.

For the first two years of internment, the main employment of the A.B.C. girls had been picking worms and rice weevils out of the daily camp food supply. As the protein level fell, people suggested leaving the insects in to enhance the nutritional value of the food. In any case, no matter how thoroughly the rice was cleaned, there were still numerous tiny insects in every mouthful. Most of the internees had long ceased to notice them. After the decision to stop cleaning the weevils from the grain, the main job of the A.B.C. girls became picking out the abundant dirt and debris, small rocks, pebbles, and other odds and ends to be found in each new shipment.

"Mom and I were cleaning rice one afternoon when Jimmy walked up with a few of his friends and showed us a large piece of shrapnel that he had found embedded in a wall near the camp kitchen. Some of the other boys had smaller pieces of shrapnel in their hands. I knew that shrapnel had been found in the camp, but until then I hadn't seen it up close. I was both fascinated and frightened."

A new awareness of their position became evident. Even if the Japanese decided to let them live to be liberated, and when, and if, the Americans arrived, Santo Tomas would instantly lose its privileged position as a POW camp full of noncombatants. The niceties of the Geneva Convention couldn't be counted on to deflect shrapnel or machine gun bullets or stray anti-aircraft shells. The camp would be right in the middle of a combat zone.

Gene leaned over the wooden table and admired the eight Camel cigarette butts, drying in the sun. In front of him lay the makings of three potential American cigarettes.

"I was wandering the campus with my brother one day and we came across an area where somebody had been smoking Camel cigarettes. We could tell the brand from the butts on the ground. Jimmy and I guessed that since tobacco was almost nonexistent in the camp, especially American cigarettes, that the cigarettes likely belonged to the Japanese or someone who had visited them recently. At any rate, I scooped up the butts from the ground and Jimmy and I decided to bring the cigarette butts to our parents.

"Dad and Mom were pleased, as we knew they would be. From the beginning of our internment, cigarettes and tobacco ran out quickly, and most internees who smoked had to scrounge the ground for the occasional cigarette butt dropped by the Japanese guards, or the fortunate few internees who could barter and trade for cigarettes. For my parents, it seemed like forever since they had a cigarette, let alone an American cigarette. Dad started shredding the butts into a neat pile of dry tobacco on the table, and then removed his battered bible from his cloth bag around his neck.

"My mother said, 'Gene! Haven't you got anything else to roll with? You know how that gives me the creeps!'

"Dad had used his bible pages for rolling paper before, and Mom always flinched when he did that. He began using only the blank sheets of paper that would be at the beginning and end of the bible, but eventually he was left with the actual printed pages.

"Dad flipped the bible open and looked at the first page he came to. He read it out loud. It was from the Psalm of David, Psalm 37:

'The steps of a man are established by the Lord, and He delights in his way. When he falls, he will not be hurled headlong, because the Lord is the One who holds his hand. I have been young and now I am old, yet I have not seen the righteous forsaken or his descendants begging for bread.'

"Dad paused for a moment and then said, 'I guess I'll use the next page.'"

Gene Faggiano was a man who didn't go looking for trouble, but if it came his way, he wasn't one to shirk away from it, either. He was a man of principle, and his earliest lessons to Jimmy and Jean-Marie included having pride in what you do and not being afraid to stick up for yourself, your family, or your beliefs. Gene was a man who could handily defend himself in trouble, having been trained as a boxer before the war and winning more than a few bouts with men his size and weight. Gene was an easy-going man, but not a man you wanted to push too far.

One afternoon, Jimmy and his father were strolling along by the Main Building when Gene spotted one of the internees that he had grown to despise. The man was a professional gambler, a racketeer, and a nipa hut slumlord. He looked fit and well fed because he was. He, and a few entrepreneurs among the Japanese guards, had made major sums over the preceding year. Business boomed with every decrease in rations. Wedding rings, gold watches, and other expensive items had come out of their hiding places to be traded for camotes and taro flour, peanuts, and tinned milk. The profits they made went back into the market to buy smuggled bootleg cigarettes and other commodities.

"The man made a comment to Dad, and I believe it had something to do with Dad being Italian. It was enough for Dad, especially with Jimmy right there. Dad didn't usually let things like this bother him, but this guy had provoked Dad before. He was just that kind of person, and this last comment was the straw that broke the camel's back. Dad told the guy he couldn't hear what he said to him from so far away, and invited the guy to come closer and say it to his face.

"Now, mind you, this guy probably outweighed Dad by over fifty pounds, most of which was solid muscle. He strutted towards my father without hesitation. Dad was no match for this guy. My father could barely keep his pants up, he was so skinny."

Jimmy had begged his father not to fight him, but Gene was not going to budge to this guy. He had seen this guy taunt and intimidate other internees, and they had all taken it. Gene told his son to stand back and watch this loud mouth get what was coming to him.

"As the fight began, Dad got the worst of it right away. The guy waded in without a word, and knocked Dad's toothpick arms aside and nailed him in the stomach with his fist. The guy then hit Dad in the jaw with an uppercut, and Dad hit the ground. At that moment, people in the gathering crowd started yelling at the guy to leave Dad alone. The guy was holding Dad up by the shirt and began taunting the crowd. It was in that space of perhaps a few seconds when Dad's reflexes took over. He brought his knee up into the guy's testicles and the guy dropped to the ground like a sack of potatoes."

Unfortunately for Gene, it wasn't enough. The guy slowly got up and smashed Gene in the face with a devastating series of blows. Gene flew backward like a rag doll, smashing into the wall of the Main Building and sliding to his knees. Gene tried his best to defend himself, but his already emaciated condition made holding his arms up impossible now. The guy pummeled him repeatedly, and then, while Gene was on the ground, rubbed his face in a spot on the ground where someone had thrown some disinfectant lye water. Gene felt the lye dissolve into his eyes and screamed in pain. At that moment, the internee police arrived and broke up the fight. When they asked Gene if he was all right, he cried, "I'm blind... oh, God help me... I can't see... PLEASE, JESUS GOD, SOMEBODY HELP ME!"

"It seemed like forever before Mom came out of the hospital and sat down with Jimmy and me and told us the news. Her face seemed cut from gray stone. She said, 'Your father is all right. He has a very bad chemical burn in his eyes. He's going to be in the hospital for a couple of days before you can visit him. He might lose one of his eyes.' Jimmy and I stared at her, taking this in, trying to imagine our father with one of his eyes gone.

"I'll never forget the look on my brother's face at that moment. Jimmy had tears in his eyes, but there was a frightening look on his face, too. His eyes were cold and distant when he said, 'I'm going to kill that guy. I'm going to steal a Jap bayonet and I'm going to run it through his heart.' Mom and I looked at Jimmy. He wasn't speaking in tones of childish bravado. He was deadly serious. I felt a shiver go up my spine, and I believe my mother felt it too. Jimmy was capable of murder. I thought, 'Dear God, what's happening to us?'"

Eileen, Jimmy, and Jean-Marie spent most of the next three days with their father, running errands for him, keeping the rag over his eye wet with cold water. His face was swollen and puffy, his one visible eye so badly inflamed that no white had shown at all. After three days he emerged from the hospital, joking and laughing with his wife and children. But they could tell that something had changed in him. The beating had hurt him more than physically. He was trying to hide the wounds of injured pride, trying to be the man he was a lifetime ago, back in 1941.

The vision in his left eye was still in question. The doctor hadn't been hopeful, and Gene wouldn't know the outcome for another several weeks.

During the latter days of November, air raids over Manila grew less frequent and then stopped altogether. Gradually, life at Santo Tomas settled back into the old patterns. War rumors began to become murky and uncertain, contradictory. Days added up and turned into weeks. The prospect of liberation faded with each food line and roll call, with each new reduction in rations. News of the outside gradually became less important than thoughts of food and day-to-day survival.

Typhus had broken out in the city, and farmers were refusing to bring what was left of their meager crops to market. In the afternoon shadows of abandoned storefronts, here and there among the unattended jungles of the public parks, unburied corpses lay rotting. Funerals secretively passed each other in the empty streets. The Japanese had become vindictive and vicious, no longer making any pretense of being the liberators of the Filipinos. Underground activity increased and so did the reign of military terror and savage mass reprisal.

If the war lasted much longer, Manila would be transformed from a metropolis to a necropolis.

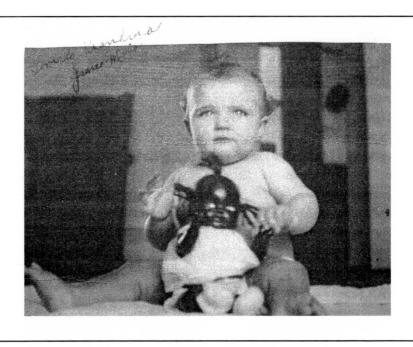

Jean-Marie Faggiano, one year old, Shanghai, China, 1936.

Jean-Marie, getting a ride in a rickshaw in Hong Kong, 1937.

Jean-Marie and her mother, Eileen (right), along with Jean-Marie's second cousin, Eugenia Connell. Hong Kong, 1937.

Jean-Marie in Cebu,
Philippines, 1937.

Jean-Marie and Jimmy, Cebu,
Philippines, 1939.

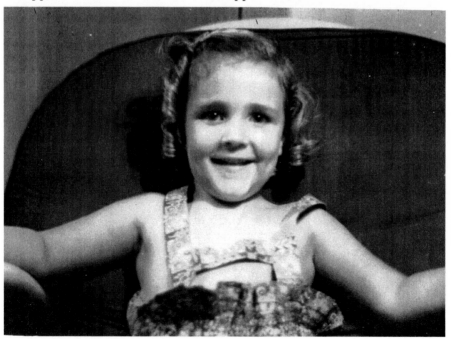

Jean-Marie, age five, in Baguio, Philippines, 1940.

Bataan Death March, Philippines, 1942. (Courtesy of the Library of Congress)

The front gate of Santo Tomas Internment Camp. Jean-Marie's father, Gene, and another internee were tortured near this location. (Courtesy of the National Archives)

Main building of Santo Tomas Internment Camp. (Courtesy of the National Archives)

Education building of Santo Tomas Internment Camp. (Courtesy of the National Archives)

Chow line, Santo Tomas Internment Camp. (Courtesy of the National Archives)

General Douglas MacArthur makes his triumphant return to Leyte, Philippines, October 20, 1944. (Courtesy of the National Archives)

Shanties in the interior area of the Main building. (Courtesy of the National Archives)

Manila, February 4, 1945. (Courtesy of the National Archives)

Men internees after liberation, February 1945. (Courtesy of the National Archives)

General MacArthur visits with internees in the Main building, February 6, 1945. (Courtesy of the National Archives)

General MacArthur waves at internees, February 10, 1945. (Courtesy of the National Archives)

Celebration in front of Main building, February 1945. (Courtesy of the National Archives)

Main building celebration. Jimmy Faggiano is in the lower left corner, wearing a striped shirt. (Courtesy of the National Archives)

Children playing on tanks, shortly after liberation, February 1945. (Courtesy of the National Archives)

Jean-Marie and Private Tanner, February 1945. (Courtesy of Stars and Stripes magazine)

Pendleton "Bumblebee" Thompson, one of Jean-Marie's closest friends in the Santo Tomas Internment Camp. This picture was taken after the liberation aboard the S.S. Jean Lafitte, bound for the United States in April 1945. (Courtesy of the National Archives)

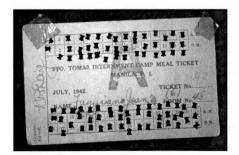

Jean-Marie's meal ticket.

Artist sketch of Jean-Marie in
Santo Tomas, 1943.

Jean-Marie's baby book, made
by a nurse at St. Luke's Hospital,
Philippines.

Eileen's bra, made by Eileen with
string found in the camp during
the last year of internment in
1944. Eileen weighed less than
eighty pounds at this time.

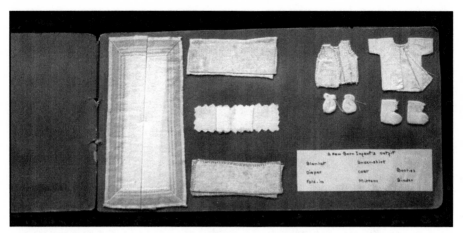

Inside Jean-Marie's baby book. All of these miniature clothes were handmade.

Apron made by Eileen during internment at Santo Tomas.

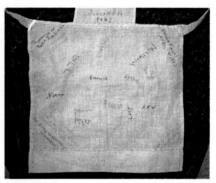

Close-up of apron, showing names of Jean-Marie's friends, teachers, and important events.

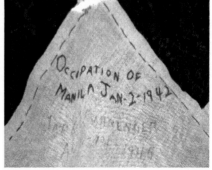

Apron close-up: "Occupation of Manila Jan-2-1942" and "Japs
85 Surrender Aug-14-1945"

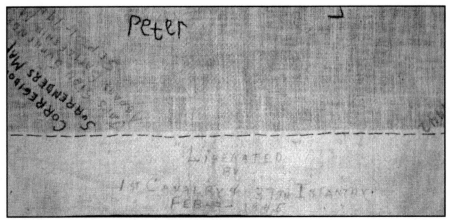

Apron close-up: "Liberated By 1st Cavalry & 37th Infantry Feb-3-1945"

Apron close-up: "Corregidor Surrenders May-6-1942" and "Japs Sign Surrender Papers Aboard Battleship Missouri Sept-1-1945" (Actual date was September 2, 1945)

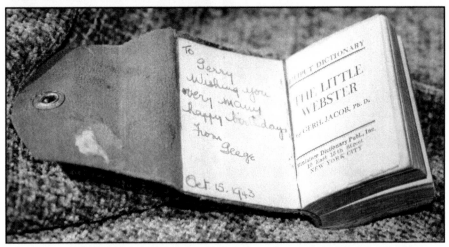

Miniature dictionary given to Jean-Marie on her 8th birthday, October 15, 1943, by her friend, Geege Wooten. Jean-Marie developed the nickname "Jerry" in the camp, and she still uses that nickname today.

A custom declaration tag on a package sent to Santo Tomas for Jean-Marie, from her grandmother in California. Jean-Marie's grandmother owned an ice cream store in San Rafael.

Jean-Marie's First Communion prayer book and cards, while interned at Santo Tomas.

Prayer book for Jean-Marie, signed by the Montinola girls; Lulu, Teresita, and Alice. Notice the rubber stamp from the Japanese on the inside cover.

Doll made by Eileen for her daughter, Jean-Marie, during internment at Santo Tomas.

A personalized card made for Jean-Marie from two internee friends of the Faggiano family, 1943.

With some help from her mother, Jean-Marie made this pouch for her father while interned at Santo Tomas. Gene used to keep his possessions in this pouch, including his multi-purpose Gillette razor.

Jean-Marie's hair, during internment in 1944 (below) and after internment in 1949 (above).

Eugene Faggiano, San Rafael,
California, 1948.

Eileen Faggiano, San Rafael,
California, 1948.

James Faggiano, San Rafael,
California, 1948.

Jean-Marie Faggiano, San Rafael,
California, 1948.

Jean-Marie playing it up for the camera, San Rafael, California, 1948.

Jean-Marie, as a teenager, at the Faggiano residence on Lincoln Avenue in San Rafael, California.

Eileen and Jean-Marie, in front of their house on Lincoln Avenue in San Rafael, California, 1949.

Gene loved all sports, including hunting and fishing. Marin County, California, 1949.

Jean-Marie at her parent's house on Linda Avenue in San Rafael, California, early 1950's.

Eileen and Gene Faggiano, with their dog, Casey. San Rafael, California, early 1950's.

20 YEARS AGO

For the first time since he was taken a prisoner by the Japanese more than three years ago and interned in Santo Tomas, word has been received from Eugene Faggiano by his parents, Mr. and Mrs. Joseph Faggiano of San Rafael. Interned with the former San Rafaelite were his wife, Aileen, and their two children, Jeanne Marie, now 9, and James Rogers, who is 11 years old.

Newspaper clipping from the Marin Independent Journal.

Jean-Marie, in the mid-1970's.

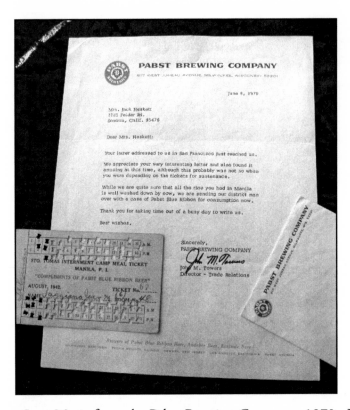

A letter to Jean-Marie from the Pabst Brewing Company, 1970. Many of the meal tickets at Santo Tomas had the words "Compliments of Pabst Blue Ribbon Beer" printed on them. Years after Jean-Marie was back in the U.S., she wrote a letter to the Pabst Brewing Company and received this letter plus a case of beer from the brewery. The letter reads: "Dear Mrs. Heskett. Your letter addressed to us in San Francisco just reached us. We appreciate your very interesting letter and also found it amusing at this time, although this was probably not so when you were depending on the tickets for sustenance. While we are quite sure that all the rice you had in Manila is well washed down by now, we are sending our district man over with a case of Pabst Blue Ribbon for consumption now. Thanks for taking time out of a busy day to write us. Best wishes. Sincerely, Pabst Brewing Company, John M. Towers, Director – Trade Relations"

Jean-Marie with her second husband, Jack Heskett, in 1975. Jack was a USAAF pilot during WWII, flying missions over Burma.

Jean-Marie and Sergio Montinola, Manila, Philippines, March 2008. Jean-Marie and Sergio are standing in the park across the street from the Montinola home on Del Pilar.

The Malate church as it looks today. The Faggiano family lived a block away from the church on Del Pilar, and attended church every Sunday before their internment at Santo Tomas.

IN MEMORY OF THE COLUM BAN FATHERS PATRICK KELLY, S.S.C. JOHN HENAGHAN S.S.C. JOHN LALOR, S.S.C. PETER FALLON, S.S.C. AND JOSEPH MONAGHAN, S.S.C., AND TENS OF THOUSANDS OF MALATE PARISHIONERS WHO WERE VIC TIMS OF THE ATROCITIES OF THE JAPANESE IMPERIAL FOR- CES AND AMERICAN SHELLING DURING THE BATTLE FOR MA- NILA FROM FEBRUARY 3 TO 17, 1945.
THIS MARKER WAS INSTAL- LED PURSUANT TO BOARD RE- SOLUTION NO.2, s.1994 OF THE NATIONAL HISTORICAL INSTI- TUTE.

Plaque outside the Malate church.

Jean-Marie, Sergio and Michael approach the Main building at Santo Tomas University, March 2008. It had been over sixty years since Jean-Marie had left Santo Tomas.

The shanty area today, from the interior of the Main building, March 2008.

The Gymnasium building as it looks today, as seen from the Main building.

The Seminary building as it looks today, as seen from the Main building.

A Santo Tomas University Museum display picture of the Annex building. The Annex building has been replaced by newer buildings on the campus.

Maita Oebanda, collection management and documentation assistant at the University of Santo Tomas, as well as curator of the Museum of Arts and Sciences inside the Main building. Maita was the tour guide for Jean-Marie and her family when they visited the Santo Tomas University in March of 2008.

Elvira Magsambol, Michael McCoy, Jean-Marie, and Angela McCoy. This picture was taken inside the Main building, March 2008.

A display board in the University of Santo Tomas museum, listing the names of the internees at Santo Tomas. The Faggiano family can be seen in the middle.

The Faggiano's were tenants of the Montinola family prior to the war. Although the house no longer stands, this is the location where the Montinola's and Faggiano's lived on Del Pilar Street in Manila.

From left to right: Sergio Montinola; Jean-Marie; Sergio and Ching's daughter, Gina; Ching Montinola; Elvira Magsambol; Michael McCoy; and Angela McCoy. Manila, 2008.

Jean-Marie at the Manila American Cemetery and Memorial, March 2008.

Jean-Marie saying prayers at the Manila American Cemetery and Memorial, March 2008.

Sergio, Elvira and Jean-Marie, in front of the Malacanan Presidential Palace in Manila, March 2008.

Jean-Marie at the president's podium, Malacanan Palace, Manila, March 2008.

Jean-Marie's reunion with one of the "Montinola girls," Alice, in Manila. March 2008.

Jean-Marie reunites with Teresita, Carmen, and Sergio.

A commemorative plaque on the wall of the Main building of Santo Tomas today. It reads: "Santo Tomas Internment Camp, Through these portals passed up to ten thousand Americans and other nationals of the free world who were interned within these walls by the Japanese military, suffering great physical privation and national humiliation from January 4, 1942, until liberated Februry [*sic*] 3, 1945, by the American forces under General Douglas MacArthur. February 1954. American Association of the Philippines"

Jean-Marie at the end of her Philippine trip, at a luxury hotel in Manila, March 2008.

Jean-Marie, surrounded by her children. From left to right: Patrick Heskett, Jack Heskett, Kathleen Heskett, Shannon Zito, Tim Heskett, and Michael McCoy. Santa Rosa, California, Christmas, 2001.

The doll that was given to Jean-Marie from Private Tanner, as it looks today.

Chapter Seven

December 1944

The Faggiano's were taking a late afternoon walk one day when they passed their garden area. Gene was talking to his family about one of the women who had a constant problem with the boundaries of her neighbor's garden plots. It seemed like she was always accusing someone of picking her talinum or taro bulbs. Just as they were about to leave the garden, their attention was drawn by a long, low whistle coming from the direction of the Calle Noval. Gene searched anxiously for the invisible whistler, but there was no one to be seen on the street behind the camp's barrier of bamboo and barbed wire. The Faggiano's stood in the deepening twilight, dark shadows amidst the rows of the empty field, listening as the hidden whistler began a melody that none of them had heard in three years. Eileen strained to recall the name of the haunting refrain. It was just on the tip of her memory. With a shock, she realized that she had forgotten the name of "The Star Spangled Banner."

With Jean-Marie leading the way, the family walked closer to the perimeter bordering Calle Noval, searching for their hidden friend. The whistling ended just as the Faggiano's reached an area ten feet from the wall. The street was empty and silent, except for an evening breeze that made the palms that lined Calle Noval rustle with a sound like the patter of a gentle rain.

Suddenly, a small Filipino boy, his wide smile flashing in the gathering darkness, stepped from behind one of the palm trees and waved at the motionless shadows in the garden. He pulled his arm back behind his head and pitched something over the wall. Once, twice, three times. The boy softly called out one word, "Mabuhay!" and vanished.

"We searched the ground and finally found what the boy had thrown over the wall. There were two green calamancis, which are Filipino small limes, and a ripe papaya. Dad used his Gillette razor to slice the two limes in half, so that each of us got our own piece. I think I must've spent an entire minute just looking at the lime, taking in the sight of the fruit in my hand. The scent of the citrus tickled my nostrils and made me sneeze.

Everyone started laughing. I bit into the lime and instantly felt the juice surging against my swollen gums, bathing my mouth in a cool fire. It actually made me gasp out loud. Looking at Mom, Dad, and Jimmy, though, I could tell they were experiencing the same sensation.

"After we polished off the last fragment of the lime, we went through the entire ritual again with the papaya. I had my slice topped off with a sprinkle of rock salt, my favorite way of eating papaya. Rock salt was the one thing the Japanese had given us in abundance, and Mom had a bag of it stored away under her bed.

"We would never know the Filipino boy who whistled the national anthem and gave us the fruit, but we never forgot his act of kindness and the small pleasure it gave our family that day. Dad just shook his head and started getting a little misty-eyed. I asked him what was wrong, and he said, 'Well, I guess I'll never stop being amazed by the Filipino people. Here they are, experiencing their own brand of hell outside the gates of the camp, and yet this young man risks his life coming to the wall and giving fruit to complete strangers.' Mom smiled at Dad and said, 'He probably sees and hears things that we can't, Gene. And maybe he knows that the end of all of this is coming soon, for both of us. I think he was giving us more than fruit. I think he was also giving us hope.'"

Eileen had been having pains in her kidneys, which forced her to move slowly, slightly bent at the waist. Consequently, Jean-Marie found herself doing more of her mother's chores, beating the bedbugs out of the mattresses, washing the laundry, and pitching in with mopping the floor of their room in the Annex.

"We were all aware of our declining physical strength in the camp, but it didn't really dawn on me how weak I had become until the day I was helping Mrs. Muir in the Main Building. She asked me to get some water for her so that she could mop one of the floors. I went to pick up a bucket of water, containing perhaps a half gallon, and as soon as I tried to lift it, it felt like the bucket had been nailed to the floor. It was beyond the limits of my strength. I might as well have tried to tow a battleship with my teeth.

Lifting a half gallon of water wasn't supposed to be this difficult, especially for a nine year old girl. I was stunned at my weakness."

Eileen was saddened by the look on her daughter's face. Jean-Marie had always seemed so spunky and full of life, but looking down at her now, she realized they were all, even the children, living right out over the edge. One unlucky Japanese edict, one unfortunate bombing mistake, and their story would be over. For the first time, she admitted to herself that there was a time limit. She mentally calculated the odds, trying to come up with an unbiased appraisal of the situation. Even if there was no major disaster, at this rate she figured that she and Gene could probably last another six months. That's about the limit. Hopefully, the children could hold on for a year, maybe more.

Eileen had been noticing, as was every last internee, her own daily deterioration. Physically, mentally, and morally, she felt she was sliding downhill. Just clinging on to life itself had become a moment to moment struggle. With two children to protect and defend, she consciously culti-vated her hatred of the Japanese and a sense of outrage at her life of imprison-onment, knowing these were the only tools left available to keep her sane and spiritually strong. With mounting horror, she saw the spreading apa-thy in the camp. The last months had drained much of the internee's ability to respond emotionally to their environment. They had been battered and bashed, catapulted time after time between breathless hope and crushing despondence. The stress was taking its toll. The ones who simply gave up, those who slowly let the fires of their identity go out, were the ones to leave the camp in the funeral cart.

Jean-Marie and Eileen woke up startled, not sure what had broken them out of a deep sleep. All the women in the room were sitting up in bed, silent and listening. One of the smaller children began to cry. Two rifle shots rang out, sharp, cracking reports echoing off the facade of the Main Building. A guard angrily shouted something, another answered. Women began to get out of their cots and move cautiously through the darkened room toward the windows. Jean-Marie followed a pace behind her mother.

"I was peeking out the window, standing between Mom and little Jean Muir. Looking out the window into the campus, I saw a guard with a hurricane lantern leading the way, followed by a squad of five soldiers. The soldiers were prodding a young Filipino man to a trot at the point of their bayonets. The prisoner was barefoot and bloody, his hands wired together behind his back. They were taking him to the main gate, and I knew this wasn't good. The last guard to pass the Annex looked at our window and, noticing us watching, raised his rifle toward the Annex. We instantly got away from the windows.

"After a few minutes we began to talk about what we thought had just happened. We knew the first guy was a Filipino, so he wasn't an internee. Maybe he was part of the underground. Some of the women began wondering if he hadn't broken into the camp to get food from the Japanese bodega. Was it possible that the food situation outside the gates had become worse than inside the gates? We knew the Filipino's were having it rough outside the walls of Santo Tomas, but we had no idea how bad things were.

On the morning of the sixth of December, internees were greeted with the distant sounds of an air raid, the first in almost three weeks. The rolling thunder of the bombing seemed to shatter the tired dream that had descended over guards and POWs alike. A Japanese staff car screeched to a halt outside Hayashi's office. Noncommissioned officers were sent scurrying in all directions. Suddenly, rows of drab army tents were struck, equipment was packed, orders were given, weapons were issued, and men began to form up in columns. Japanese troops filed out of their quarters and into the central plaza.

A convoy of heavy army trucks arrived, and Santo Tomas was quickly stripped of military supplies, leaving only a few machine guns and light mortars for the defense of the camp. A second convoy stayed only long enough for the combat troops to pile on board. They rumbled off through the main gate, leaving over a hundred guards, twice as many as before.

That evening, while the internees were at roll call, their rooms were thoroughly searched. All books and magazines were confiscated, as were all sharp instruments, bolo knives, and straight razor blades. The internees had learned, through long experience, that the guards could be trusted not to steal anything from their rooms. Even the lowliest troops were remarkably disciplined. If ordered to search for a radio, they would search for a radio and a radio only, ignoring anything else that might come to light, even obviously illegal items.

The internees knew their rooms would be disordered, their possessions scattered on the floor and jumbled together, but all their precious junk, down to the last hoarded can of Spam, would be there on their return. When a guard stole from an internee, he did it in an outright, straightforward fashion, with an infuriating smirk of invulnerability and a sarcastic "domo arigato."

A number of announcements were made. All library books had to be resubmitted for censorship by members of the commandant's staff. Curfew was now to be seven o'clock at night with lights out by eight. Half the light bulbs in the camp were to be confiscated for use by the army.

Starting in the middle of the night and continuing throughout the day, elements of the Japanese Fourteenth Area Army had been moving up the Calle Espana, headed for their fortified positions in the mountains outside Manila. Light air raids were taking place north of the city. As the internees lined up for their morning mush, the combined noise of the armored traffic and the muffled bomb detonations stirred their hopes for a speedy deliverance. It seemed the Japanese might well be in the process of abandoning the defense of Manila. Rumors ran rife through the camp regarding an American landing in Batangas, a town on the southern tip of Luzon. By the middle of the day, these rumors had been checked out via the garbage detail and had proved to be false. The rumor had raised high hopes because of the heavy Japanese traffic. Once again, hopes were quickly dashed.

In growing resignation and despair, the internees began to accustom themselves to the idea of spending yet another Christmas in captivity. In contrast to the two previous years, almost nobody had the endurance or the inclination to prepare a program of holiday festivities for 1944. Another starving Christmas season, existing at the unpredictable whim of their jailers, was widely viewed as nothing to celebrate. The only thing they had to look forward to, aside from the problematical arrival of the American army, was the usual Christmas distribution of Red Cross packages. According to the arrangements made between the Tokyo government and the Red

Cross, internees were supposed to receive one relief package a month. In actuality, they received one a year. This was the typical Japanese army modus operandi, all too familiar to the internees of Santo Tomas. On a dozen different occasions, the executive committee had spent hours in conference with the commandant and his staff, reaching all sorts of dandy agreements, even written ones, to find that in practice the Japanese habitually ignored all agreements, acting as if they had never taken place.

The question of whether they would receive this year's parcel was of paramount importance. There were hundreds of seriously ill internees to whom the Red Cross supplies would mean the difference between life and death. The all-important Red Cross parcel weighed eleven pounds and contained the following: dried fruit, Spam, canned fish, cheese, crackers, margarine, dried milk, soap, cigarettes, and chocolate. The internees, forcing down their rice paste with weevils, were aware that mountains of these packages were piled in storage sheds on the docks of Manila, earmarked for use by Japanese combat troops. The question of whether any fraction of these supplies would be released for distribution at Santo Tomas caused more controversy than a Presidential election was capable of generating back home in the states.

During the second week of December the air raids grew in intensity until the sky north of the city was never without its attacking formations of American bombers, barrages of Japanese defensive anti-aircraft shells, and the heavy dark covering of burning oil.

Jean-Marie noticed Jimmy crouched, sneaking Indian-fashion between the rows of garbage cans outside the guard's bodega. Jean-Marie had already checked the cans and knew Jimmy wouldn't find anything remotely appetizing. Now that the guards were starving along with the internees, the quality of their garbage had fallen appallingly. Jean-Marie came up quietly behind Jimmy, and then pounced, swatting him over the head with her rag doll. Her brother cried out and whipped around to see who was there. Seeing it was only his obnoxious kid sister, he clutched her by the arm and dragged her down to kneel by his side. Jimmy thrust his mouth next to her ear and whispered between clenched teeth, "Shhh! Stay out of sight!"

"Jimmy was on to something, and soon I found out what all of his sneakiness was about. I peeked around the side of the garbage can and found that I was able to see into a back portion of the Japanese kitchen. A Japanese soldier was emptying a bucket of coconut pulp into a soaking trough. I had gotten a glimpse of this device the year before. The soaking trough was basically a heavy wooden box on concrete legs. Coconut pulp would be fed into a hole in the thick wooden planks that formed the top of the box. The coconut would then float, soaking and softening in water that was filled to within six inches of the top of the box. Jimmy and I watched as several buckets of pulp were emptied into the trough. After a few minutes, the guard wandered off toward the front of the bodega. There were no other Japanese in sight.

"As usual, my brother tried goading me into getting some of the coconuts. Jimmy rationalized that since he found it, I should go get it. I told him he must be crazy if he thought I was actually going to sneak into the Japanese kitchen, but he countered by calling me a chicken. He kept daring me, but I wouldn't give in. Then he double dared me. That did it, as usual. Next thing I knew, I was heading for the kitchen."

Once inside, Jean-Marie froze against the gritty inner surface of the sawali kitchen wall, holding her breath and straining her ears to catch a hint of trouble. It was only a yard to the soaking trough, but to her, the mission objective seemed as far off as the dark side of the moon. From another part of the bodega she could hear the Japanese cooks talking among themselves, rattling pots and pans. For a moment, she almost made up her mind to play it safe and duck out the door and run. She turned to do exactly that, but the first thing she saw was Jimmy, still crouched behind the garbage, urgently signaling her to hurry up and proceed.

In two strides, Jean-Marie was at the soaking trough, her hand down the hole, clutching frantically at the slippery coconut pulp that seemed to have an innate talent for evading her grasping, grubby little fingers. After heart-stopping moments of suspense, she was finally able to wrap her hand around three large pieces of yummy, juicy, coconut.

"And then I heard it. The sound I dreaded to hear most of all: 'HUH-HH!!' I spun around to see the guard charging down a narrow hallway towards me. I tried to pull my hand out of the trough, but it wouldn't come. I tugged with all my strength. No good. Something was preventing me from freeing my hand. The guard was fast approaching. I pulled with all my strength, and could feel the skin ripping around my wrist. I was going crazy with panic."

Jean-Marie realized that if she opened her fist, she could free her hand from the hole in the trough. Just a fraction of a second prior to this, in her state of panic, the thought hadn't even occurred to her. She had the prize in her hands, and that was all that counted. Now it was gone. The coconut pulps dropped back into the trough with a splash, as Jean-Marie opened her hand and leapt backwards, stumbling toward the door. Another half second and the guard would have caught her.

"I have run pretty fast in my time, but this time I don't think my feet even hit the ground. I actually think I was flying. I headed for the Annex by way of about a dozen zigzag patterns around the other buildings of the camp. When I was finally confident that the guard had given up his pursuit, I snuck back to the Annex. In reality, he probably gave up long before I quit running, perhaps even as soon as I left the kitchen, but my adrenaline level and fear wouldn't let me stop running. It was only when I had finally arrived at the Annex that I was able to catch my breath and let the whole incident sink in. I never saw Jimmy in all of the excitement. He apparently saw the guard coming at me and ran off ahead of me, with probably just as much speed."

Dr. Theodore Stevenson was the internee head of the hospital at Santo Tomas. While working on his weekly medical report, the second for December, he took in the latest statistics. The death rate was climbing sharply in the over sixty category. The elderly, combined with the total from all other age groups, made the first two weeks of the month the worst in the history of the camp. Eleven internees had taken the death cart ride out of Santo Tomas, including an eight year old girl who had died of tubercular meningitis, an infant boy with pneumonia, three elderly men in the sixty-five to seventy age group -- one from a cerebral hemorrhage and two from coronary thrombosis -- and a middle-aged woman from encephalitis.

Included on Dr. Stevenson's list was another death, a teenage girl that had succumbed from malnutrition. In the past, whenever Dr. Stevenson had listed malnutrition as a cause of death, it had thrown the various Japanese administrations into a fury. He had been called out on the commandant's carpet and was quickly persuaded that it was in everybody's best interest to list the death as "natural causes." Stevenson knew the girl had been overwhelmed by a combination of bronchitis and malaria. With the required medicine and diet, Dr. Stevenson had no doubt the child would have recovered. It was essentially the lack of nutritional food that had killed her.

"Dad went back to Dr. Stevenson for a checkup on his eyes in December. During the checkup, Dr. Stevenson told Dad about all of the false 'natural causes' that he had recorded before for people that had actually died of malnutrition. He said the teenage girl was the last straw for him. He told Dad that if the Japanese didn't like the idea of a young girl's blood on their hands, then they can damn well feed us some decent food."

December 15, 1944
To the Commander-in-Chief
Imperial Japanese Army
In the Philippines
Through the Commandant, Philippine Internment Camp #1

Sir:

In August and September of this year, Medical and Dental surveys were made of the children in this camp. The Medical survey, which covered 800 out of the 835 children from three to nineteen years of age, showed that 63.5% of the children are underweight, with one quarter of this group very seriously underweight (15-20% underweight). The Dental survey, which covered 697 out of the 835 children from three to nineteen years of age, showed that 63% of the children have defective teeth.

In comparison with normal figures, these percentages are so alarming that we feel compelled to address this letter to the highest authority available to us. Our Health Council believes that the serious degree of underweight and the high percentage of defective teeth are due principally to lack of essential items in the children's diet.

All the efforts which have been made by the previous Japanese administrations and by the parents to provide the children with supplemental food out of limited funds have proved inadequate to prevent this under nutrition. This has been especially true of the last six months, during which time the Japanese army has reduced the official ration (of which children under ten years of age are allowed only one half) from a bare maintenance to a starvation level.

It will soon be impossible to furnish the children with any supplemental food at all, either by the camp or by the parents themselves. This means that the children will be limited to the food allowance supplied by the Japanese army. This allowance provides no eggs, no milk, no fruit, and none, or absolutely insufficient quantities of many other items essential for the children's subsistence. This is bound to result in an even more appalling condition among the children, and, we fear, in death or permanent physical impairment for many. This can only be avoided if the present Japanese food allowance is increased and supplemented.

Therefore, we ask that the children be given and adequate ration which will include sufficient quantities of corn, vegetables, fruit, meat, and the following essential items:

One egg per day per child

One pint of milk per day per child up to six years of age

One half pint of milk per day per child from six to eighteen years of age

Three bananas per day per child

One half kilo of peanuts or peanut butter per child per week

In requesting the above, we believe we are asking for nothing which present conditions make impossible. All these items are produced in or near Manila in large quantities. From information given to the internees in this camp by a Japanese official who had been interned in the United States, we know that the Japanese children there are being especially well cared for. Therefore, we request that steps be taken immediately to provide reciprocal treatment for our children. We cannot reconcile the traditional Japanese love for children with the treatment being accorded to the children in this camp.

Signed on behalf of the 932 parents of children interned in Philippine internment camp #1.

The Parent's Committee

A.E. Holland, Chairman

It was an oppressive, sickly sweet hot morning, humidity making the air seem thick and difficult to breathe. Jean-Marie looked forward with yearning for the time of the afternoon rains, the most beautiful moment of her day. About two o'clock, like clockwork, the glaring blue of the sky would start to undergo a weird polarization, growing visibly darker by the moment. Then a surging, dark gray wall of heat-spawned clouds would roll across the horizon, its deep interior lit by jagged and darting flashes of forked lightning. For a little while, the breathless heat would become even more stifling. Then, in one sudden outburst, the clouds would empty themselves, sending thundering sheets of water down to the waiting earth below.

The rainfall was still hours away when Jean-Marie first heard the rumble. She suddenly became aware of the far off sound of airplane engines. She supposed the air raid siren would go off soon, but didn't bother to look up, since flights of airplanes were passing overhead several times a day. Then she noticed the windows of the Annex filling with spectators, and the nearby Japanese leaning out of the guard houses with expressions of astonishment.

"I looked up and squinted into the hazy, white glare, and caught sight of a huge air armada covering the sky from horizon to horizon, as far as the eye could see. I tried to count the number of aircraft, but quickly lost track. I had never seen so many planes in the sky at once."

Wedge after wedge of bombers and swarming wasp-like clouds of fighter escorts cruised serenely above the furthest limits of the flak, tens of thousands of feet over the camp, headed for the waterfront districts and the northern air fields. The planes were at the peak limit of their altitudes, barely discernible above the cloud cover. For ten minutes, there was no break in their ranks. Wing after wing, squadron after squadron, they paraded unopposed across the Manila skies in a staggering display of power.

The first flights began pounding the docks, and yet the sky was still filled with ranks of advancing American aircraft. It was the air raid to dwarf all previous air raids. Grinning internees went about their tasks to the morally uplifting music of continuous carpet bombing, crashing and rolling across the city from the direction of the harbor.

Long after curfew, the women of Eileen and Jean-Marie's room continued to sit silently by the window, staring out at the massive destruction of a city they all knew well. Gushing, towering gouts of flame colored their faces a dark rose. This was bombing on a high order of magnitude. None of them had seen or imagined anything on this scale. Previous raids had cheered and encouraged them, whispered congratulations floated across the vegetable garden or between the mosquito nets for every dive and strafing run on the totally outclassed Japanese. But the spectacle before them that night transcended all of that, and was utterly beyond all vindictive thoughts of winning or losing, beyond all personal considerations. Entire sections of the city had been blown into splintered rubble, and then set ablaze with incendiary clusters. The most severe raids to date had been relatively isolated in the selection of targets, concentrating on one strategic location or another. This night's raid, however, had been an apocalypse, a curse falling on the heads of the sinful.

Carroll Grinnell was the chairman of the Internee Executive Committee, one of the most important and influential internee officials, and as such was one of the few internees in camp to have access to a typewriter. Christmas was fast approaching, and discussions had begun among the various groups -- the Parent's Committee, the Entertainment Committee, and the Internee Committee -- as to how to make the holiday season as merry as possible. After all concerned had pooled their resources, they had been forced to admit there wasn't much to be done. Compared with previous years, they had almost nothing to work with. Grinnell decided to type a letter to enlist the help of others to help plan whatever they could.

December 20, 1944
NOTICE TO ALL BUILDING AND FLOOR MONITORS AND
AREA SUPERVISORS:
CHRISTMAS EXTRAS
The camp has on hand a quantity of jam and chocolate which it is proposed to distribute to internees for Christmas. There are two possibilities of distribution for each of these extras, and the Internee Committee wishes to

have, by Friday at the latest, a general survey by rooms and sections stating the number of internees in favor of each suggestion:

A. JAM: Either-
1. Serve the jam on Christmas Eve through the canteen on the basis of one 2 lb. tin of jam for three canteen cards, i.e. 18 people, or

2. Mix the jam with a number of green papayas available from the camp gardens, cooking the two together and serving them at the same time as the mush on Christmas morning. The quantity served to internees would thereby be increased by the amount of green papaya included in the jam.

B. CHOCOLATE: Either-
1. Serve on Christmas Eve through the Canteen, nine 30-gram rolls of chocolate for three cards, i.e. 18 people (15 grams per person), or

2. Mix the chocolate with the lugao on Christmas Day and serve the chocolate lugao for lunch to the whole camp.

(Signed) CC Grinnell
Chairman
Internee Committee

Carroll Grinnell would never know how the "Christmas Extras" would go. Three days later, on December 23, Grinnell, along with three other members of the Executive Committee -- Alfred "Dug" Duggleby, Ernest Johnson, and Clifford Larsen -- were arrested. All four had been accused by the Japanese of being involved in various ways with the underground, smuggling food and medicine into the camp. In the following month, the four would be led out the front gate, taken away and executed, never to be seen again.

The arrest of the Internee Committee was accompanied by the most extensive and most destructive search in the history of the camp. Bowing to the scowling, enraged guards, seeing their meager property smashed and scattered about, the internees prepared their souls for the worst. It seemed the Japanese were planning to retaliate for the massive air raids, taking revenge against the only targets close at hand. The fear of sudden, violent death gripped the camp, putting the prisoners through a night of almost unbearable tension.

On the morning of Christmas day, the entire camp received an unexpected present. American planes had dropped leaflets over Santo Tomas. The first internees to discover them lying soggy on the dew covered ground, snatched them up and hid them away in their clothes, then went striding happily back to the major population centers where thousands of people would be standing in bathroom lines and getting ready for roll call. Within an hour, every internee had received their season's greetings.

"The Commander-in-Chief, the Officers, and the men of the American Forces of Liberation in the Pacific wish their gallant allies, the People of the Philippines, all the blessings of Christmas, and the realization of their fervent hopes for the New Year. Christmas, 1944."

Chapter Eight

January 1945

"We spent New Year's day much like many of the internees, visiting each other's quarters and wishing everyone a happy new year. Many adults would celebrate by sipping burnt soybean coffee and pretending it was champagne. Spirits were generally pretty high, in spite of the worsening situation inside the camp. I think many of us really believed we were in the home stretch. I remember hundreds of Filipinos had turned up at the main gate, bearing presents and food for all of the prisoners, but they had been sent away by the guards on the Calle Espana.

"Dad seemed to be in a particularly good mood. He looked better than I'd seen him in awhile, and I think most of that was just his high spirits shining through. He did worry about Mom, though, and Jimmy and I shared that concern. Mom was having serious kidney trouble and was reduced to shuffling along, bent over quite a bit. Dr. Stevenson had explained that a needed layer of fat surrounding her kidneys had melted away, leaving them without support. He had improvised a back brace for her to help her walk, and Dad helped her with chores that she found too difficult to do. Mom, being Mom, still managed to keep her spirits in tune with Dad's, and I think she found his optimism encouraging. She worried about him a lot over the course of this past year, especially after the fight and his eye injuries. But Dad was doing better, and he was sure our liberation was coming soon. The sky continued to be full of huge American bombers, and his eyesight was almost completely clear. He was feeling more hopeful than ever, and I was glad to see it."

A few days later, Gene and another internee nicknamed Red were on a work detail, moving sacks of rice onto a cart. Suddenly, both men froze in place, hands still on the rice sacks, faces turned toward the roar of engines. Three P-51 fighters burst over the northern wall of the camp at low level.

Gene was excited and lost himself in the moment. He could feel the adrenaline rush through his veins. He stood astride the rice sacks and raised his fists into the air, transported by the beautiful sight of the fighters, and yelled "YAHOOOOOOOOOOOO!"

Red was also excited, but quickly warned Gene to quiet down. Red remembered what the commandant had said about cheering American planes. But Red's warning came too late. Two Japanese guards had seen and heard the cheer. As they approached the men, one of the guards had his rifle aimed at Gene's heart. The guard gestured with a crooked finger.

"YOU. Come."

Gene managed to make a face of surprised innocence.

"What...me?"

"Hai! You come!"

Gene climbed gingerly down off the rice sacks. This could be trouble. Red chose that unfortunate moment to speak.

"I tried to tell you, Gene. You should have kept your mouth shut!"

The guard turned and regarded Red with a cold, accusatory stare.

"YOU... you come too!"

"ME? I didn't..."

"YOU COME!"

"I knew right away that something terrible had happened. Whatever the news was, it had to be really bad. Just the look on Mom's face said it all. Seeing how frantic she was made my own terror leap several levels in intensity. Mom was the kind of person that didn't get shaken easily, but whatever she knew was making her tremble. The look in her eyes was one of absolute fear.

"She said, 'Your father's been taken to the main gate.'

"Immediately, I felt an icy chill run down my spine. We all knew what this usually meant. Jimmy and I asked her what had happened, and she said she didn't know, that they wouldn't tell her.

"She grabbed our hands and led us across the campus at a fast walk. While walking, Mom told us that she had been to Hayashi's office a dozen times, and the only thing she could find out was that Dad wasn't alone, that some other internee with red hair had been taken out the gate with him. Mom said she had to do something for Dad or they'd kill him. She marched us towards Hayashi's office."

Hayashi had ordered the two men to stand at attention outside the main gate and stare into the sun for several hours. Hayashi didn't feel the sentence was unduly harsh. In fact, he was acting in a perfectly humane fashion, letting them off easy. In comparison to methods being used outside the walls, he felt the internees of Santo Tomas were still being shamelessly coddled. Hayashi knew at Fort Santiago the administration wouldn't just make prisoners stare into the sun. They'd chain them to sheets of corrugated tin and leave them to fry.

"Mom was in the commandant's office, standing before Lieutenant Colonel Hayashi and his interpreter. Jimmy and I were standing outside, looking through the window. Through his interpreter, Hayashi told Mom that Dad and his friend had broken a very serious rule and had to be punished. He told her that we were very lucky that he didn't inform the military police. Mom begged Hayashi to reconsider. She explained that Dad was a very sick man, and that his eyesight was recently injured and wasn't fully healed."

Eileen sensed that the critical moment had arrived. Hayashi rattled his papers, coughed irritably, and made other unmistakable gestures to indicate that he was rapidly growing annoyed. Eileen was well aware that any Japanese male, let alone a ranking officer, hated to be opposed, contradicted, or questioned by a woman. Time was running out.

"Mom finally begged Hayashi to look out his window at her two young children, Jimmy and me. She asked the commandant how we were going to live with a blind father. Then she asked him to have mercy on his children and commute the sentence to time in jail, instead of the punishment outside the main gate."

Eileen lost all hope. It was obvious that Hayashi had heard enough. His features grew hard and he hissed his answer at the translator. He didn't once glance out the office window, where Jean-Marie and Jimmy were standing at formal attention, as if posed for a school photo.

"We went to the Internee Committee next, and they said there was nothing they could do. If Hayashi hadn't bended with Mom, he wasn't going to bend with them. Mom blew up, as I knew she would. She yelled at the Committee until her voice went hoarse. She sat down on the ground and put her head in her hands."

"For the first time since we entered the gates of Santo Tomas, I watched my mother cry."

It was not quite ten in the morning as they took their places outside the main gate, balancing on the curb of the Calle Espana. As soon as Gene looked up at the sun, he knew he'd never survive. The glaring light, stabbing scarlet arrows into his barely healed eyes, was an assault worse than a physical blow, bypassing the outer surface defenses and exploding in the deepest part of his brain. The most brutal beating would be better than this. After an hour of balancing on the narrow concrete curb, staring into the monstrous noon sun, Gene was ready to throw himself on the bayonet. His eyes were flashing with blinding, throbbing waves of agony. Gene could imagine his eyes roasting and sizzling in their sockets, precious eyesight dripping down his cheeks in a clear stream of molten pain. He staggered forward off the curb, and instantly angry voices rang in his ear, screaming out incomprehensible sounds in some unknown, grating language. Hands seized and repositioned him on the curb with slaps and kicks. A center of cold sensation spread in the middle of his back. Dimly, Gene recognized that he was being propped up with the point of a bayonet. He was momentarily amazed, as his body seemed to regain its balance and straighten up on its own, with no effort from his will or mind. His body wasn't ready to give up. With or without him, it intended to fight for life.

Gene caught a blurred glimpse of Red standing a few yards away. Nearby, under the shade of a parasol, a Japanese guard was dozing, curled up in a broken, rattan lawn chair. For a moment, Gene felt a stab of guilt for having gotten Red involved. Then the guards watching Gene grabbed his hair and jerked his head back. The blast furnace of the demon sun instantly washed all thought away. He felt his brain screaming inside his skull, shriveling, charring, and turning into steam. Nausea gripped him and he vomited a thin gruel down the front of his filthy shirt. One of the guards standing at the gate nudged his buddy in the ribs and pointed to the two stooped, pathetic skeletons attempting to stay balanced on the narrow curb. The prisoners were both babbling to themselves, holding animated conversations with the thin air.

Passing the early afternoon hours in the shade of the guardhouse, watching the two Americans slowly losing their minds, one of the gate guards had a brainstorm. Within an hour, a dozen of his messmates had placed their bets and were busily figuring the odds on which of the two prisoners would drop first. In placing this bet, a variety of factors had to be wisely considered, and the guards were loudly arguing the fine points of the contest.

Gene had been wearing a shirt at the time of his arrest, whereas Red had been stripped to the waist and was fully exposed to the sun. Gene was Italian and swarthy. Red was Irish and fair. However, Red was bigger and stronger. Both men were near collapse, and one or the other could fall at any moment. By two o'clock all bets were in, and the group of guards waited intently for one of the two men to buckle and drop. The babbling had stopped, and both had been silent for almost an hour.

Red suddenly collapsed onto the sidewalk. It took the guards several minutes to slap him awake and stand him back on his feet. The sun was dipping down to the horizon, turning from a blazing white to a mellow golden bronze. Red collapsed again, for the last time, and the bets were paid off.

Hours went by, and the air cooled with the gentle breezes of the coming twilight. The crazy one was still on his feet, now whispering furiously under his breath. The guard had lost heavily on Red. He figured someone so big and strong would be the one still standing. Anyway, in another half hour the sun would dip below the horizon, his relief would arrive, and he would stroll across campus to the bodega and get his dinner. Idly wondering if his bet was still alive, he ambled over to the lobster red body and gave it a prod in the back with his bayonet. A low moan broke from Red's blistered lips. His curiosity satisfied, the guard stared at Gene for a moment, then turned and sauntered back to the gate.

The last ray of sunlight dropped below the horizon, officially ending the day. The instant the sun disappeared from the sky, Lieutenant Abiko ordered two privates to get a stretcher and carry Red to the internee hospital. The guard behind Gene gave him a nudge with his bayonet. Unsteady on his feet, Gene promptly collapsed to the sidewalk.

After several attempts, Gene was finally revived. He crawled on his stomach, blindly groping his way back to the main gate, guided now and then by savage kicks in the ribs. Eileen watched with helpless horror, as what was left of her husband inched closer through the deepening twilight. She wasn't allowed to touch him until he dragged himself across the threshold of the gate.

Gene was in the camp infirmary, suffering from severe exhaustion, shock, sunburn, dehydration, and damage to his retinas. He had bandages over both of his eyes. Eileen stayed by his side, wiping the fevered sweat off his forehead. On the morning of the second day, as Eileen laid a cool rag across his eyes, Gene began to come around. Jean-Marie and Jimmy sat silently in a corner of the clinic.

"Mom was saying, 'Gene, are you awake? It's me, Eileen. Gene! Gene, talk to me! Are you awake? It's me, Eileen.'

"When Dad finally awoke, he mumbled to Mom, 'Eileen, I don't want... to be buried here... at Santo Tomas... I want to be buried... in the States.'

"Mom was shocked and asked him what he was talking about.

'I've had it, Eileen. I'm through... I can't go on anymore.'

"Mom stared at him with a fury that was beyond all words. She slowly raised her arm and jabbed a rigid, accusing finger at Dad.

'EUGENE FAGGIANO! Don't you DARE die and leave me here with these two kids!'

"Dad didn't say another word about dying after that. Mom wouldn't hear any of it. She was being tough for Dad, reminding me of the way he used to be so tough for us. She was angry at him, but after a moment or two, she leaned over, put her arms around him and started humming a tune to him. It was a song that they used to dance to at the Manila Hotel. 'Moonlight Serenade' by Glen Miller. It was their song.

By the time Dr. Stevenson came down the hall and joined Eileen, Gene was sound asleep.

Jean-Marie watched from a safe distance as the commandant's office was emptied of its files. Continuous processions of soldiers were carrying heavy cardboard boxes from the office and dumping the documents in an oil drum, where they would then sprinkle them with gasoline, drop a match into the barrel, and duck under the first gushing fireball. Once the fire subsided, they would stir it thoroughly with an iron stake until the papers were reduced to ash.

"I had spent almost every waking hour inside the clinic with Dad, and as much as I loved him, it was good to be outdoors again. The clinic was full of very sick and dying internees, either scrawny with wasting diseases like jaundice or tuberculosis, or bloated with beriberi. The stench was terrible. To our relief, Dr. Stevenson had declared that Dad wasn't going to die, and he wasn't going to be blind, but he wasn't getting out of bed either, not for at least another two weeks.

"I enjoyed watching the Japanese burning the documents, because for a kid my age, it was exciting hearing the huge 'whooooosh' sound that came from the igniting of the gasoline and the big ball of flame that followed. I was too young at the time, though, to understand the bigger interest the adult internees seemed to have in this whole thing. I had seen the adults nudging each other in the ribs, gesturing at the commandant's office with knowing nods, and shaking hands in congratulations all morning long.

"I finally asked Mom about it, and she told me that the Japanese obviously had papers that they didn't want anyone to see. I asked Mom what that meant, and she said it meant that they were either preparing to leave or just didn't want any evidence of something left around after the camp was taken over by the Americans. Either way, it seemed to be a promising sight. One thing was clear: they were sure in a hurry to get rid of it, whatever it was."

A new edict had been ordained, decreed, and declared. All internees would henceforth be confined to quarters during air raids, allowed to go about their business only if and when the "all clear" signal was given. Persons performing essential services, like medical workers, garbage detail crews, and kitchen workers, would be exempt. In as much as the tempo of the air attacks had picked up, this meant that a major portion of each day was spent in the dank, stale, mental pressure cookers of the main buildings. Hours would pass in the Annex when hardly a word was uttered. Internees and guards alike, sapped of their vitality, were rapidly losing ground on the sustenance provided by one skimpy meal of starch a day. The guards had slaughtered and consumed their last pigs and ducks. They stripped their own extensive vegetable plots, and then made a clean sweep of the internee gardens.

Weeks of constant air attacks had sandpapered the nerves of the Japanese soldiers down to the snapping point. The bombing was taking place on the northern or western horizons, the American airplanes far out of the range of any weapon at Santo Tomas. Day after day the troops manned their positions, crouched uselessly behind their guns while American aerial attacks transformed railroads, shipyards, airfields, piers, refineries, supply dumps, factories, and thousands of young Japanese men, into part of the looming gray-green shroud of ash and acrid smoke that had become a permanent fixture over Manila Bay. Long convoys of men, supplies, and material were constantly passing the camp on their way to defensive positions in the mountains.

It's likely that the Japanese at Santo Tomas were feeling like the last men on a sinking ship. Their famous discipline was slipping, crumbling incrementally. Many of the guards had ceased to wash or shave. The Americans had occupied Luzon in force, and were pushing in a triple pincer movement toward Manila. It wouldn't be long before they impacted against the city's outer defenses. The rules that had governed the camp behavior for three years began to lose importance in the minds of guards and internees alike. Although it was still necessary to bow to the officers, especially Hayashi and Abiko, internees gradually realized they could stop bowing to privates. The privates ignored them, no longer concerned with what the prisoners did or didn't do. They had bigger problems. A tidal wave was approaching, and there was no way off the beach.

The first "all clear" signal didn't sound until almost noon. Within minutes, thousands of hungry internees poured out of the buildings, eager to stretch their legs and shake off the oppressive feeling of stagnation and confinement. Jean-Marie, Jimmy, and Bonnie charged for the front of the breakfast line, collected their lugao breakfast, and were already licking their tin plates while the rest of the camp was still lining up to be served. There was no time to waste. The camp was alive, electric with excitement. Something was happening, and Jean-Marie was burning with curiosity to find out what it was.

For as long as she could remember, Santo Tomas had been like a sleepy little village. A baseball game might be the major event of the week. Men would actually sit and watch while their friends got haircuts. Even the air raids and the progress of the war had become commonplace, in a category with the weather. Now, she and her friend Bonnie could barely keep track of all the activity taking place on campus. The Japanese and various internee squads had been hard at work since dawn. Trucks and cars had been rolling in and out of the main gate. Officers were rushing from building to building with sheaves of paper in their hands. The camp was in turmoil. Long forgotten supply sheds were being opened, and their moldy contents, tools, mattresses, clothing, and ammo, loaded onto waiting trucks. Barrels of gasoline, having been buried years before in the first days of the occupation, were dug up and loaded for transport.

Jean-Marie and Jimmy headed for the main focus of activity, which was taking place in the rear of the camp. Normally a quiet, out of the way location, that corner of the camp was swarming with trucks and troops today. The children watched as one of the Japanese trucks pulled its tailgate up to the door of a supply shed, where guards were waiting impatiently to load thousands of entrenching tools. As they opened the flap to the back of the truck, they recoiled in consternation and demanded that the driver get out and explain what was going on. The driver peered into the back of the truck, did a double take and checked the invoice list on his clipboard. The leader of the squad and the driver almost came to blows before Lieutenant Abiko stalked over and demanded to know what was going on. Moments later, soldiers were dumping the truck's cargo by the side of the road, a load of antique furniture looted from the best homes in Manila. Porcelain vases exploded against carved seventeenth century teak and mahogany. Intricate patterns of veneer, lovingly polished for two hundred years, were gashed and mangled, huge mirrors shivered into splinters, rosy portraits of chubby, frivolous French courtesans died with the ripping of their canvas, Venetian gild glass chandeliers were pounded flat under the weight of a massive marbled oak armoire.

An internee stepped forward, bowed, and held a brief conference with Abiko. The lieutenant listened for a moment, nodded abruptly and turned away, preoccupied with the loading of the entrenching tools. The mangled furniture, now precious firewood, was quickly carted toward the internee kitchen. The firewood shortage was a major problem. Most of the nipa huts had been stripped, and several internees had even asked permission to break up the wooden stairs and entrance to the Gymnasium.

On January 7th, members of the newly elected Executive Board had been summoned to a meeting with Commandant Hayashi at his office, and had been waiting in the commandant's outer office for over two hours. The four men had been watching the hectic pace of the Japanese activity with mounting excitement; every indication seemed to confirm that the entire force of guards and staff were preparing to abandon Santo Tomas. The committee spent the time in Hayashi's waiting room, debating the consequences of a Japanese withdrawal. The main question was whether the internees should wait inside the walls of the camp for the American advance, or should the entire population of the camp make a grand exodus for the nearest reported American position? Both options had a strong potential for disaster.

Abiko suddenly opened the door to the inner office and gestured for the men to come inside. As soon as the Executive Committee members took their seats at the table, Hayashi's interpreter informed them that the commandant had been given a new responsibility from the War Prisoners Division. The interpreter went on to explain that, as all of the board members knew, the commandant had been concentrating much of his efforts preparing the camp's defenses with the intention to wait at Santo Tomas and fight the Americans to the last man. However, in the past days he had given much thought to the presence of the women and children in the camp, who would, unavoidably, be caught in the fighting. To prevent the shedding of innocent blood, Commandant Hayashi decided that it would be better to retire to the hills and join with the Japanese Fourteenth Area Army group. The interpreter then explained that the commandant was assigning the Executive Board members the responsibility for the camp's administration until his return, or the arrival of the Americans.

The Internee Committee left Hayashi's office in stunned silence.

"Jimmy and I joined a growing circle of internees gathered around the Japanese kitchen. The adults were grinning, bubbling with quiet joy. I asked a gaunt, elderly woman what was happening, and as the woman turned to face me, I was surprised to see her face was covered with tears. She was overwhelmed with emotion and was unable to speak, so instead she pointed toward the miraculous sight of the Japanese kitchen being taken apart and carted away for loading. The point was obvious. If the Japanese were taking apart their kitchen, they must be leaving. Jimmy and I ran to tell our parents the news. Before long, the news spread until every internee was aware that our captors were preparing to evacuate Santo Tomas."

Two days later, on January 9th, Abiko again summoned the Internee Committee to the commandant's office, where he abruptly informed them that there had been a change in plans. Just as the thrilling news seemed certain and the full force of wild joy began to break loose, the commandant's loudspeaker crackled, sputtered, and then, in a few short sentences, dashed the hopes of every internee at Santo Tomas into the dirt.

Shortly afterwards, the Internee Committee posted the following:

NOTICE FOR BROADCAST:

This morning, immediately after roll call, the Commandant summoned the Internee Committee and instructed them to make the following announcement to all internees:

So that the camp may not become the scene of bloodshed endangering the lives of the internees, the Commandant and his staff had planned to move to another place. Since such a condition has not arisen, the Commandant and his staff are staying. His anxiety for the welfare of the internees leads him to make public the following:

1. The Commandant's immediate concern is primarily in connection with food. It is almost impossible to find any food in the city of Manila, but the Commandant and his staff will make every effort to secure any food which can be found.

2. It is essential that we should make the fullest use of facilities within the camp, and every effort must be made to keep the gardens going at full capacity.

Signed,

The Internee Committee, acting in the continued absence of the executive board.

On January 9th, the same morning that the internees got the news that the Japanese were staying at Santo Tomas, General MacArthur was ready to lead the men of the U.S. Sixth Army in a landing at Lingayen Gulf, an area of sheltered beaches on the northwestern coast of Luzon. This location placed his troops close to the best roads and railways on the island, all of which ran through the central plains south to his main objective, Manila. Also, by landing that far north of the capital, MacArthur allowed himself maneuvering room for the large force he intended to use on Luzon. Once the beachhead was secure, his initial effort would focus on a southern drive to the Filipino capital. Possession of this central core, as well as Manila Bay, would allow his forces to dominate the island and make any attempts at further coordinated defenses by the Japanese exceedingly difficult. At seven o'clock that morning, the pre-assault bombardment began and was followed by the landings an hour later. With light opposition from Japanese forces, General Krueger's Sixth Army landed almost 175,000 men along a twenty-mile beachhead within a few days. It was to become the largest campaign of the Pacific War, involving more troops than the United States had used in North Africa, Italy, or southern France.

The battle for Luzon had begun.

Sunset over Manila was staggering, with dazzling shafts of gold and ruby light refracted through galaxies of dust and ash particles, flaming, transcendent, and awesome. But Jean-Marie wasn't interested in the sunset; she was watching the two dozen Japanese soldiers riding past the Annex on bicycles, their belongings contained in small wooden chests strapped across their shoulders. This was the last remnant of the day's outbound parade, a constant procession of trucks, cars, and foot soldiers. More than half the guards had been assigned combat duty, leaving less than one hundred men to guard the camp. Leaving the relative security of Santo Tomas, the former guards rode off soundlessly into the deepening, dusky-rose twilight, passing though the main gate and into the land of the lost.

Jean-Marie lay in bed and listened to the continuous rolling roar of far off explosions. To the west, American bombers were staging an unrelenting attack on the docks. To the south, Japanese demolition squads were at work in the city, torching the Cavite oil reserves, bridges, the shipyards at Navotas and Malabon, the Caloocan railroad yards, the telephone exchange, and anything that might be useful to the advancing enemy.

"I heard the sound of an airplane in distress -- the missing, sputtering drone of a bomber engine -- flying in low near the camp. I sprang to my feet and ran to the window, followed by a handful of women. We searched the skies for the source of the noise, which was becoming louder by the second. Then, directly in front of us, we caught sight of an American B-29 bomber with flames coming from its wings. I saw some of the airmen jump from the plane, as the bomber, engulfed in a searing fireball, dropped to the ground and exploded somewhere to the north. As I watched the parachutes open, I noticed that one of them didn't. This man was plummeting to earth. I kept waiting for his parachute to open, but he kept falling. I watched him drop all the way to the ground below, and I felt a wave of grief engulf me. I began to cry. That scene shook me to the core, and even though I had seen death before, for some reason this scene haunted me. I went to bed that night and couldn't sleep, my mind kept racing with the possible scenarios that could've taken place for this brave man. Was he already dead? I prayed that this was the case, because if he wasn't and was struggling to open his chute, that would have been horrible. Perhaps he was killed by Japanese bullets on his way down. I just didn't know. But I felt this incredible sadness for him. I ended up crying myself to sleep."

Dr. Stevenson stood before Commandant Hayashi and his interpreter. The interpreter told the doctor that the commandant was extremely distressed by his groundless accusations, and for the last time, he had an opportunity to rectify all of his mistaken entries on the death certificates. Further, he stated that this was a most generous offer from Commandant Hayashi, and he begged him to consider his position carefully before he chose to answer.

Stevenson realized he could either retract his statement or stick by his guns. The new interpreter was far more formidable than the run-of-the-mill mediocrity that had, over the years, characterized the staff of the commandant. He spoke flawless English and seemed to be able to read between the lines. The possibility occurred to Stevenson that the new interpreter was a Kempeitai agent, sent to infiltrate the camp's underground communications.

Dr. Stevenson told the interpreter to please convey to the commandant his regrets, but he would not change his findings.

The interpreter asked Stevenson if he was aware that his lies constituted an insult to Commandant Hayashi, to the Imperial Japanese Army, and therefore an insult to the Emperor. He again insisted that Stevenson change the reports.

Dr. Stevenson began to argue about the direness of the food situation, but Hayashi would hear none of it, arguing that the Japanese soldiers were getting the same rations as the internees. Again, Stevenson protested, admitting that although it was true that the soldiers were now on reduced rations, the internees had been enduring a substandard diet for the last three years. He was about to go on when he was once again interrupted by Hayashi. The commandant tore the death certificates into pieces and ordered new ones to be issued.

Dr. Stevenson refused to fill out new death certificates, saying that if the diet of the internees wasn't drastically altered for the better, then many more death certificates would bear the same diagnosis.

Dr. Stevenson was arrested and sentenced to jail for the next several days.

From the beginning of the landing at Lingayen Gulf, MacArthur was unhappy with the pace of the advance. He personally drove up and down the advancing line, inspecting units and making suggestions. After visiting the Thirty-Seventh Division, as it advanced south from San Fernando to Calumpit, MacArthur sent off a message to General Krueger criticizing "the noticeable lack of drive and aggressive initiative."

On the 31st of January, MacArthur toured the liberated Cabanatuan POW camp, fifty miles northeast of Manila. MacArthur had received underground intelligence reports over the years, but never in his darkest moments could he have imagined the true nature of conditions at Cabanatuan. Walking through the reeking haze of the barracks, shaking hands with one cadaverous inmate after another, MacArthur had to constantly fight back both his rage and his tears. He never dreamed what the survivors of Corregidor and Bataan, his boys, were experiencing. The harrowing actuality overwhelmed him. Standing in the camp cemetery, surrounded by shallow, unmarked mass graves, MacArthur summoned one of his most trusted and competent officers, Major General Verne D. Mudge of the First Cavalry. Mudge had fought by MacArthur's side through campaign after brutal campaign. Together they had seen the ultimate horrors of war, but Mudge couldn't remember ever seeing "the American Caesar" so shaken. MacArthur was thinking of the slaughter at the Palawan POW camp. Almost two hundred Americans had been herded into a pit, doused with gasoline, and set alight. Those that tried to escape the flames were machine-gunned to death. There had only been a handful of survivors to tell the tale.

MacArthur knew he had to move, and move fast. He had received intelligence from military code-breakers that a message from Tokyo to field commanders in the Philippines gave strict orders to not only kill all military prisoners before the Americans could liberate them, but the civilians as well. The army had also received a message from an internee transmitter inside Santo Tomas that said that it appeared that the Japanese were preparing to execute the prisoners. There was no time to wait.

MacArthur turned to Mudge, gripped his shoulder and gave him his orders.

"Go to Manila. Go around the Nips, bounce off the Nips, but go to Manila. Free the internees at Santo Tomas. Verne, you've got to get there before it's too late."

Mudge formed a mechanized task force under the First Cavalry Brigade commander, Brigadier General William C. Chase, commanding two motorized cavalry squadrons, reinforced with armor and motorized artillery with support units. This "Flying Column" rushed toward Manila, while the rest of the division followed and mopped up.

Chapter Nine

February 1945

Just before noon on Saturday, February 3rd, a low-flying American fighter plane approached the camp from the north. The plane came screaming out of the clouds and dived directly for the center of the Santo Tomas campus. The flashing fighter streaked down to within a hundred feet of the ground. As the plane approached, the "stars and bars" under its wings grew bigger and brighter, and the face of the pilot became clear. The fighter pulled out of the dive at the last moment and, with engines roaring, soared into the sky. Before it did, a small object fell from the plane to the ground, landing in one of the courtyards of the Main Building.

An American internee by the name of Paul Danner located the object and picked it up. It was a pair of brown leather pilot's goggles with a note wrapped inside one of the concave lenses. Written on the note were the words: "Roll out the barrel! Christmas is coming today or tomorrow!"

That evening, internees stared out the windows or lay in their cots, listening to the rattle of machine guns and small arms fire that echoed through the streets surrounding Santo Tomas. For months, the war had been a spectator event taking place miles away on the horizon. Now, the camp seemed to be at the center of the cyclone. Eileen and her roommates huddled closer together; their children snuggled protectively into their laps as they discussed the potentialities of an uncertain future. It was evident that the events of the next few days would decide their fate.

At approximately nine o'clock that evening, the internees of Santo Tomas were bedding down for the night when they heard a loud explosion suddenly erupt from nearby, followed by a sustained, deafening burst of machine gun fire. For a moment, the clanking rumble of tank treads could be heard, but this clamor merged and was drowned out by a booming thunder of crashing impact and the sounds of a mighty engine revving against resistance.

Suddenly the firing stopped and a voice called out, "Where the hell is the front gate?"

The voice was American, loud and clear. A staccato volley of rifle shots rang out, coming from the direction of the Japanese bodega.

"We sprang to our feet, mothers clutching their children, and ran to the window of the Annex, straining to see through the darkness. A large, dark shape had moved onto the campus from the Calle Espana, lurching and churning over the broken rubble of the gate complex, a pair of blazing searchlights sweeping over the buildings of the campus.

"It was a tank. Oh, my God, a tank. At first we didn't know if it was American or Japanese, so we became scared that the tank would fire at us and blow us up. But soon it was obvious that the tank was an American tank, as the lead tank sent up a cluster of rocket flares, illuminating the camp with a harsh, white, phosphorous burst of glaring light. We could see that the first tank was followed by at least three others, and they were all American. We were all stunned. 'Sweet Jesus God Almighty,' my mother said. And that was all she could say right then. We were numb with relief and joy. We were going to be liberated! Oh, thank you, God! The Americans are here for us!"

Lines of infantry men crouched by the sides of the hulking armor, and moved cautiously forward across the campus, taking a defensive position in the main plaza. The Annex emptied in a mad, headlong rush. Jean-Marie ran barefoot outside, swept along by a rushing tide of women and children surging toward the main plaza. From every building a stream of internees converged on the American soldiers, ignoring the crack of single rifle shots that continued to sound out from Japanese positions in the camp.

Within minutes, thousands of cheering men, women, and children surrounded their liberators in a laughing, sobbing, deliriously and hysterically happy mob that hugged them, kissed them, grabbed them, and hoisted them onto their shoulders.

"I was knocked this way and that, reeling in the glare of the tank headlights. I could only catch glimpses of the soldiers, but I realized that they were unlike any men I could remember. They were huge! They seemed three times bigger than the guards or the internees. I fought to get closer to the middle of the crowd. I had to be near them!"

Someone started to sing the first words to "God Bless America." In moments, thousands were joyfully singing at the top of their lungs. In the midst of the celebration, the commander of the lead tank threw open his main hatch and stood on top of the gun turret.

"ALL YOU PEOPLE! GET BACK IN THE BUILDINGS! GET BACK IN THE BUILDINGS!"

In the outer glare of the searchlights, the head of the internee committee and two Japanese officers were advancing slowly toward the tanks with their hands up. Infantrymen disarmed the two Japanese officers, taking their swords and pistols and thoroughly searching them for concealed weapons, while the internees shouted threats and insults. An escort of soldiers led them through the hostile crowd and presented them to the American commander, Brigadier General William Chase. The general asked where the commandant was, and through a translator, was told that Hayashi was holed up in the Education Building with over two hundred hostages, demanding safe passage out of the camp.

General Chase considered his next move. He only had two hundred men and five tanks. Reinforcements couldn't be expected until morning. If the Japanese counterattacked in force, his men would be overrun and the camp population massacred.

The general and his men were distracted by a sudden howl of anger coming from the fringes of the crowd. Lieutenant Abiko, his hands on top of his head, was walking forward through the crowd of internees. In spite of the spittle flying into his face, the weak blows and deadly insults aimed at him, he was smiling serenely, advancing toward the tanks at the center of the crowd with firm, decisive strides. When he had come within a few yards of the American commander, Abiko suddenly took his hands off his head and reached for something over his shoulder. Instantly, one of the officers opened up with his carbine, stitching bullets across Abiko's chest and belly. When they searched him, they found a pouch on Abiko's shoulder that contained a grenade. Abiko had thought to catch the Americans with this simple trick, but they had seen this ploy and others far more ingenious dozens of times before.

According to Jean-Marie, Abiko was still alive when he was dragged into the lobby of the Main Building.

"He was lying on the floor, surrounded by people who had excellent reasons to want him dead. I watched as internees took turns kicking and spitting on him. Several women even burned him with cigarettes. I moved closer to the scene, when suddenly I felt someone grab me from behind and roughly pull me backwards. It was my mother, and she was angry. She scolded me for watching and quickly led me away. I remember thinking that if anyone should want to see this man suffer, it would be my mother. But she didn't, and she didn't want me to be a party to it, either. She told me, 'There is already enough hatred for this man. We don't need to contribute more. You don't have to forget, but you have to let the hate go. Otherwise, you'll carry it around on your shoulders like garbage for the rest of your life.' Although I didn't understand it at the time, over the years I've grown to understand what she meant. It's advice that I've passed on to my children as well."

An hour later, Abiko was dead.

Back out on the campus, havoc was breaking loose. Hidden groups of Japanese were firing toward the American position as the GIs herded the internees back into the buildings. Tanks began to break the formation in the main plaza and rumble in the direction of the Education Building. Four tanks took up position in front of the building, their searchlights moving back and forth across the windows. Unknown to the Japanese, dug in on the second and third floors, internees trapped in the Education Building were signaling to GIs located on the roof of the Main Building, revealing the enemy location.

After a prolonged period of shouted negotiations, General Chase called out for the hostages to move to the rear of the building. Suddenly, his tanks opened up on the first floor where they knew no hostages were being held, riddling the walls with heavy caliber machine guns and punching huge holes in the concrete with cannon fire. This attack was followed by long minutes of silence while the Japanese spread out, taking up positions at the windows and ordering the hostages to lie down on the floor. While the Japanese guards were occupied in the fire fight, a dozen internees managed to escape by tying bedding together and sliding out the rear windows of the third floor. Two of the men, either too old or too weak to hold on to the improvised rope, fell most of the way, critically injuring themselves.

The fight at the Education Building was just beginning.

Hardly anyone slept that night. Sporadic firing came from the Education Building as rounds of shouted negotiations ended in a deadlock and more combat. Hayashi had ordered barricades blocking the stairwells and the doorways, effectively cutting off all hope of rescue for the hostages. Several of the hostages were wounded during the night. Another handful managed to escape by climbing out the rear windows of the second floor. In other parts of the campus, GIs combed the buildings, the supply sheds, the bodegas and kitchens, capturing about thirty guards in the process. Cannons boomed, machine guns chattered, and sniper fire crossed the campus, with stray shots ricocheting in all directions.

Before dawn broke, the GIs who had been stationed at the building exits finally were given the go ahead to let the internees out of their rooms. The joyous horde poured once more onto the campus to find that their familiar Santo Tomas Internment Camp had been transformed during the night into a heavily armed fortress.

The bulk of the guards were still barricaded in the Education Building with their hostages, but the rest of the camp was under American control. During the hours that the internees had been confined to their rooms, hundreds of GIs had arrived, more tanks, trucks, jeeps, armored troop carriers, and self-propelled guns. Tents were going up, fox holes were being dug, and machine gun emplacements were under construction.

"The first thing I noticed when Mom and I emerged from the Annex was a handsome young GI, stripped to the waist, shaving and washing the lather from his face from his helmet, turned upside down and filled with water. I was awestruck by how healthy he looked, and his cheerful, smiling, self-confidence. He smiled at me when he saw me, and he asked me where I was from. I told him, 'Right here, Santo Tomas.' At that moment, I really couldn't remember being from anywhere else.

"The soldier opened his k-rations and held out a thick bar of sweet chocolate. He said, 'Here, would you like some chocolate?' and before he finished his sentence, I took the candy from his hand. I think he was shocked by the way Mom and I tore into the chocolate, devouring the entire bar in moments. He laughed and told us both to slow down, that there was plenty more where that came from."

It was the first bite of a food frenzy that was to prove disastrous to Jean-Marie and hundreds of other internees.

Jean-Marie and Eileen made their way past the main plaza, where GIs were standing guard over a couple of dozen captured Japanese guards. The prisoners were stripped down to their loin clothes, seated cross-legged, their hands wired together behind their backs.

"An American soldier was trying to communicate with them. They wanted something and he was unable to understand what they were saying. I knew just enough Japanese, from my lessons with the Japanese boy that gave me the candied-coated almonds, to understand the words for 'cigarettes' and 'water.' I told my mother what I thought they were asking for, and she told the soldier."

Jean-Marie and her mother walked through the complex of newly erected tents, toward the Education Building where the Americans and the Japanese had reached a standoff. Hundreds of distraught people, whose fathers, brothers, sons, and husbands were trapped inside, waited at a safe distance for the outcome of the hostage drama.

Rumors had circulated through the crowd that the Japanese had already killed the hostages, or would shortly begin to. Another rumor had it that Hayashi had wired the entire building with explosives, and that his plan was to blow himself and the hostages to bits rather than face surrender. Suddenly, wild cheering broke out in the direction of the main gate as another column of tanks and trucks drove onto the campus. Soldiers were tossing canned goods and combat rations by the handful to the starving internees lining the road.

"Mom told me to wait for her, and she ran to join the crowd that was scrambling for the cans and combat rations. She fought her way to the front of the mob and bent down to pick up a can of peaches that had rolled near her feet. One of the internees behind her pushed her in an effort to get the can first. Mom fell forward and landed in the road, right in the path of an oncoming tank. I felt my heart stop as I watched her struggle to get to her feet. She was so weak, it was taking all of her strength to get up and run. Then she fell again. Along with other internees around me, I screamed for the tank driver to stop, but there was too much noise. The driver couldn't see Mom through his view slit. Suddenly, Dad appeared out of nowhere and, with another internee, dashed out to the road and grabbed

Mom. They pulled her to safety just as the tank rolled by. She was literally seconds from being crushed."

Near the camp perimeter, a young GI was on patrol with a group of other American soldiers. A Japanese guard that was hiding nearby suddenly opened fire on them. The GIs quickly returned fire, and then silence. The Japanese guard lay dead behind a large block of concrete.

Private First Class Theo Tanner, the GI who led the patrol, approached the corpse and cautiously bent down and examined the body for souvenirs. He knew full well that certain items, like weapons and flags, were frequently booby-trapped. He searched for telltale wires, and, finding none, removed the dead soldier's *senninbari* "thousand stitch belt." A small doll, now stained with its owner's blood, fell from the loosened belt to the ground. Tanner thought it was likely a gift from the soldier's daughter. He picked the doll up from the ground and stuck it in his jacket pocket.

After the soldiers worked their way into the camp, Private Tanner spotted Jean-Marie walking toward the main plaza. He thought she resembled Shirley Temple, only this girl was much thinner than the child actress back in the States. Suddenly, Private Tanner had an idea. He jogged a pace and caught up with the little girl with the curly hair.

A reporter for "Stars and Stripes" magazine, Sergeant Sam Blumenfeld, was nearby and spotted the two in conversation. What he overheard and wrote down was printed in a later issue of the magazine under the headline "A Smile in Burning Manila."

"Here little girl, this is for you."

"Oh no, I couldn't take it. It's a Japanese doll."

"C'mon...it's a present."

The little girl looked at the doll in Private Tanner's outstretched hand.

"It does have a pretty face."

"Sure it does. Why don't you take it? A doll is a doll, no matter who makes it."

"Well, okay, but I'll have to ask my grandmother if I can keep it."

"That's fine," said Tanner. "Why don't you run along now and ask her?"

"Oh, I couldn't do that," the girl said. "She's in America!"

Tanner smiled and offered her the doll again. The little girl smiled back, and this time, she reached over and took the doll from Private Tanner's hand.

At that exact moment, Sergeant Sam Blumenfeld moved his camera into position and snapped off a shot. It was a picture that he later considered one of the most special moments of his wartime experience. He never forgot the smile on that little girl's face.

As he stood up and put his camera back in its bag, he smiled and waved at Jean-Marie. She smiled back, and before he knew it, she was off running toward the main plaza again, clutching the doll in her hands.

Snipers, the object of intensive house-to-house manhunts by the American troops, were still taking pot shots from the houses surrounding the campus. Gene told his family that he heard a rumor that sniper shots had been reported from the campus Seminary Building, a building previously occupied by priests. According to a friend of Gene's, the American soldiers, going room by room and floor by floor, cleaned out a handful of snipers from the building and were shocked to discover that all of the snipers were disguised in the black robes of the priests. According to the rumor, the real priests were later found on the third floor, their stripped bodies piled in a corner of what had been a lecture room with their hands bound behind their backs and their throats cut from ear to ear.

Whether this story is true, or just another rumor that germinated from the collective hatred that many internees held toward their former captors, is unknown.

The situation at the Education Building hadn't changed, and at any time the camp could be overrun by a major Japanese counterattack, but Jean-Marie could have cared less about any of these adult problems. She felt wonderful. No matter how much she ate, she was still hungry, and, miracle of miracles, there was always more to eat.

"An open kitchen had been set up near the Annex, and Jimmy and I joined our friends and lined up and got our fill of the food being offered. We polished off several glasses of Klim powdered milk. Klim is milk spelled backwards. We also ate a big plate of bean, bacon, and hard tack. As soon as we were finished, we got right back in line for seconds. This was truly heaven!"

The GIs had hooked a radio to the camp public address system. News of the war, denied for so long, crackled forth from loudspeakers that, during the last three years, only were used to communicate the "ukase." The news was interspersed with jazz and the latest hits from the Andrews Sisters.

Every child, and many of the adults, were to be seen carrying sacks of food back to the buildings where they would lie surrounded by unthinkable delicacies: sugar, crackers, butter, jam, jelly, Klim by the bucketful, hard tack, cans of fruit cocktail, chocolate bars, chocolate powder, bacon, and dried beef.

Soon, long lines of groaning internees were forming at every available latrine.

This generosity came too late for many of the older prisoners. The lingering effects of years of starvation were killing many of them, and in spite of every effort by army doctors and nurses, and would continue to do so for weeks to come.

Japanese marine demolition teams were blasting the heart of Manila into rubble, taking a terrible toll of the city's population in the process. The Japanese marines had fortified the old walled city at the center of the downtown area, Intramuros, and were planning their last stand within the massive Spanish fortress, taking with them several thousand Filipinos as hostages. Refugees and wounded Filipinos began to flood to Santo Tomas, waiting for a chance to get medical treatment at the improvised field hospitals that were being thrown together at half a dozen locations within the camp. American troops continued to pour in, as well as Filipino families of internees, at last united with their loved ones after three long years of separation. Soon, GIs were posted to keep the flood down to a steady stream.

The situation had reversed itself; guards were needed to keep people out of Santo Tomas, rather than in.

Gradually, the internees learned that they had been liberated by a "flying column" composed of two hundred men from the famous First Cavalry and five tanks from the Forty-Fourth Tank Battalion. These men had seen action in Fiji, Guadalcanal, the Solomons, Bougainville, Leyte, and Luzon.

A hundred men had stormed the rear wall off the Calle Dapitan, while the tanks had bashed their way through the front gate. By the next morning they had been backed up by five hundred more men.

"Jimmy and I never stopped moving. The campus was in a state of confusion, but it was exciting, with never ending surprises in store. The GIs were very friendly, and would answer all of our endless questions.

"Along with some of the other children, I was given the chance to climb on their tanks, including 'Battling Basic,' the lead tank that had broken through the front gate. I was given piggyback rides, ate heaps of the GI's food, and loved it when they patted my head or tousled my blonde curls. I was madly in love with every last one of them."

In this, Jean-Marie was not alone. Moira Malone was constantly surrounded by a circle of young soldiers. Soon, all the teenage girls at Santo Tomas, as well as many of the women, had soldier boyfriends.

The Education Building standoff lasted all day Saturday, with no progress made toward releasing the hostages. Hayashi was adamant in his refusal to surrender, and made it plain that rather than give up to the Americans, he would have every last hostage killed and their bodies thrown out the windows, one by one.

Finally, on Monday morning, February 5th, a compromise was reached. General Chase sent a negotiation team into the Education Building, including one of his most trusted officers, Lieutenant Colonel Charles E. Brady, to negotiate the final arrangements face to face with Hayashi. Brady stepped out from behind the protection of "Battling Basic," squared his shoulders and walked with a firm, confident stride toward the entrance to the Education Building. Inwardly, he was feeling anything but firm and confident. He had been through a dozen island assaults, faced shot and shell, but he had never deliberately exposed himself to the point blank muzzles of enemy guns. Hundreds of internees and GIs watched as the negotiators strode across the space between the tanks and the riddled facade of the Education Building.

Hayashi, backed by half a dozen gun-toting guards, was standing in front of a barricade that blocked the hallway to the main entrance. As Brady approached the Japanese, he tried his best to keep any trace of fear out of his face. After a few minutes of talking with Hayashi, he didn't have to try anymore. His fear was replaced by a cold hatred. Hayashi made a great show of fearless pride and arrogance, sneering at the American and standing with his feet planted wide apart. All through the time spent with the American officer, Hayashi would constantly take his two pistols half way from their holsters and let them drop back in again. Brady, famous for his huge handlebar moustache with its precisely upturned points, was later to recall, "My hand twitched so badly watching that sonofabitch that I had to twirl my moustache to keep it steady."

After an hour of discussing terms, they hammered out a bargain. Hayashi and his men would be permitted to leave the camp grounds and, with a guarantee of safe conduct, they would be escorted to their own lines. They would be allowed to retain their swords, side arms, and rifles, but would have to leave their automatic weapons and hand grenades behind.

Later that morning, Commandant Hayashi led the way out of the Education Building, followed by sixty-seven guards marching three abreast. American troops, with submachine guns leveled and ready, formed two lines that flanked the Japanese column. Thousands of internees cheered as they watched the last group of Japanese march through the main gate of Santo Tomas, turned right on the Calle Espana, and disappear in the direction of downtown Manila.

Dazed internees stumbled out of the Education Building to a hero's greeting. Families rushed into the arms of their loved ones as squads of GIs entered the building and, room by room, conducted a meticulous search for mines, time bombs, and booby traps. The former hostages were escorted by a cheering crowd to the newly installed field kitchen, where the first decent meal they had seen since 1942 was waiting for them. Two internees had been wounded by machine gun fire, another had died of a heart attack, and one of the men, who had fallen during the escape attempt, later died of his injuries.

The Japanese troop contingents of Santo Tomas were safely escorted to within a block of their own line and allowed to cross over to join their comrades. Unknown to the Japanese, however, was that the area they chose to be released in was an area that was occupied by a Filipino guerilla unit. Shortly after their release by the Americans, the Japanese found themselves engaged in a firefight by the Filipinos. Most of the Japanese were killed. The surviving Japanese were captured and brought back to Santo Tomas.

Lieutenant Colonel Toshio Hayashi was among the dead.

Jean-Marie and her friends climbed out on the balcony that overlooked the entrance to the Main Building and the central plaza. Below, the plaza was jammed with internees and GIs waiting to see the colors of "Old Glory" over the scene of their ordeal. A huge American flag was suddenly unfurled from the balcony of the Main Building, right next to Jean-Marie, as people below shouted encouragement and cheered every few moments from an irrepressible feeling of sheer joy. Jimmy was watching below, wearing a striped shirt that his mother had saved for him to wear after the liberation. His chest was swollen with pride. Jean-Marie, standing on the balcony with the others near the flag, saw Jimmy and waved to him.

Softly at first, but gaining in strength and volume with every word, the former prisoners sang the national anthem, followed by "God Bless America." There were no speeches or music, no stirring words of promises for the future. The sight of their flag flying, the knowledge that they were free men and women once again, was more than the internees could handle. Hundreds of men and women burst into tears. They embraced each other and broke down sobbing helplessly in each other's arms.

To Jean-Marie, it seemed the remainder of that day was spent waiting in lines. But now, instead of receiving a miserable handful of rice mush, the head of the line would have marvelous things in store to reward a small girl's patience. Hot, delicious food, Red Cross clothes, and mail! Thousands of letters were delivered to the internees. It was almost beyond comprehension. A person could write their thoughts, without deletions, without censorship, and could actually seal the envelope without first presenting it to the authorities.

"Mom's family had written dozens of letters from Baltimore, and Dad's family from San Rafael, California, had done the same. We huddled together as a family on the steps of the Annex, opening letter after precious letter, sorting through three years of family news and events in one deliriously happy afternoon."

Jean-Marie slept through MacArthur's visit. Even if she had been awake at the time, the words "Douglas MacArthur" wouldn't have had any significance for her. The commander of the Pacific Theatre arrived at Santo Tomas early Wednesday morning, February 7th, surrounded by an entourage of bodyguards, newspaper reporters, and top army brass. MacArthur gave a short speech to an overflow crowd that jammed the lobby of the Main Building. He then circulated among the cheering crowd, shaking hands with the internees, many of whom he knew by name.

MacArthur followed in the wake of the American vanguard that had finally reached the "Genko Line" and joined battle with the Japanese marines. A house-to-house battle for Manila was raging. When it would finish, five weeks later, very little of the city would be left standing. Pockets of Japanese marines would actually hold out for a month after the city had fallen, hidden aboard some of the four hundred shipwrecks that clogged the harbor.

Jean-Marie, Jimmy, Bonnie, and Jean Muir were standing in the long lunch line, their mouths watering and their stomachs rumbling as the glorious smell of frying bacon wafted out from the environs of the field kitchen and tickled their nostrils. Each meal was still a miracle. Jean-Marie wouldn't have exchanged a meal for a nonstop ticket to heaven.

After lunch the little group of friends stuck together. Now that the camp was completely cleared of Japanese, they were free to wander at will. Jean suggested that they take a peek out the front gate, perhaps followed by a short walk down the Calle Espana. Jean-Marie still had a lingering feeling of terror associated with the main gate, and was reluctant to approach it, but Jimmy and her friends joked and jostled her until she had to admit that the front gate was now perfectly safe.

A squad of GIs were busily checking and rechecking the identity of the Filipinos who sought entrance into the camp. The refugees formed a long line that stretched down the length of the outer camp wall, and extended around the corner of the Calle Governor Forbes. On either side of the gap, where the iron gate used to be, machine gun emplacements covered the street and the crowd of refugees, ready to open fire at a moment's notice.

Jean-Marie spotted a GI near the gate and asked him if it would be okay if she took a short stroll outside. The soldier considered this for a moment, and then turned to Jean-Marie and knelt down in front of her.

"He said to me, 'Well all right... but do you see that big tree down there?' I nodded yes. He said, 'I don't want you going any further than that. I shouldn't even let you go that far, so I want you to promise me that you won't go wandering off, okay?' I nodded my head again. I walked outside the gate for the first time. It was exciting to leave the confines of the camp, but after a short while I regretted my impulse to explore the outside world. I felt exposed and vulnerable. Inside the camp I was now provided for, loved, and protected by hundreds of American guns, but outside I was only a small child walking alone through the scattered, smoldering rubble of total war. The sounds of explosions were continuous; I could feel the ground shaking under my feet. Toward the regions of the battle, the sky was a solid wall of black, billowing smoke, looming thousands of feet into the air. Every step I took away from the main gate seemed to scare me more. After walking only a few hundred feet, I couldn't tolerate the insecurity any longer. I turned back, walking at first, and then breaking into a run. I didn't stop again until I was back inside the concrete and barbed wire walls of Santo Tomas."

Jean-Marie had just stepped inside the main gate when she became aware of a piercing whistle. It reminded her of something familiar; she knew she had heard similar sounds in the distant past. Suddenly, the third floor of the Main Building burst asunder in a massive explosion, sending a cloud of concrete dust rocketing out over the plaza.

The Japanese still held the main post office, the city hall, the church of San Sebastian, and the Marco Polo Hotel. From the roofs of these buildings they rained shells down on Santo Tomas, using anti-aircraft guns, light artillery, and mortars. The artillery and anti-aircraft ordinance made a long, screaming note as they hurtled toward the campus, giving soldiers and internees plenty of time to gauge their trajectory and take cover. It was the mortar shells that fell silently, giving no warning until the moment of impact. Several internees were killed and many more wounded by the end of the day.

By late afternoon, the first barrage lifted and dazed internees went cautiously about their business, ready at any second to hurl themselves onto the ground. Batteries of howitzers were wheeled inside the campus. They quickly zeroed in on the Japanese positions, and a booming artillery duel began that was to continue for several days. Santo Tomas had become a combat zone.

In total, eighteen internees had been killed by the shelling and sixty-five were wounded. Some of the GIs and Filipino civilians in the campus had also been killed.

"After a few days the Japanese shelling had stopped, as the Americans had taken out the Japanese positions located outside the camp. Jimmy and I were hanging around one of the artillery officers in charge of one of the batteries. He told us all about the guns. We were in awe with how powerful they were. I think Jimmy was even more impressed by the big cannons than he had been by the tanks. He decided right then and there that he was going be an artillery officer when he grew up."

All the men surrounding the guns smiled sympathetically at the children's ardor. After three years of combat, they were sick of the sight of howitzers. Most of them would likely be half deaf the rest of their days.

A projector had been set up in the middle of the plaza and a motley, improvised screen of bed sheets hung from a large bamboo framework. Jean-Marie and Eileen made their way through the crowd, found Gene and Jimmy, and sat down on the ground with a multitude of others, waiting for the show to begin.

The internees were treated to an Edward R. Murrow Pathe Newsreel, "Fighting on the Russian Front." Jean-Marie watched as huge tanks churned through high banks and drifts of snow. She had entirely forgotten that such a thing as snow existed. She tried to imagine what it would be like to be surrounded by the cold, fluffy white stuff. On the screen, lines of Russian rocket launchers and cannons sent screeching salvos of shells into beleaguered German positions. The thundering sound effects of their detonation, so stirring to audiences in America, were totally drowned out by the battle of Manila, raging only two and a half miles away.

After the news came the feature film, "I Married a Witch," starring Fredric March and Veronica Lake. Jean-Marie was dazzled. The film was only three years old, a product of "the Golden Age of Hollywood." Fredric March was manly and handsome. Veronica Lake was beautiful and glamorous.

The last attraction of the evening was a concert given by the First Cavalry jazz band, "The Housatonic River Rats." To resounding applause, they worked their way through "Stompin' at the Savoy," "One O'Clock Jump," "Boogie Woogie Bugle Boy," "Moonlight Becomes You," and "Take the 'A' Train." GIs danced with the local internee talent, while a series of terrific explosions lit up the horizon.

"One day, I made the biggest mistake I could've made in the army field kitchen. I managed to get my hands on about a pound of butter, a half pound tin of jam, two wax paper cubes of hardtack, about ten cans of Spam, a pound of raw bacon, and five bars of chocolate. I was ready to have my own personal feast. I put it all in a gunny sack and went for a walk where I was more or less by myself. I opened up the sack and began to devour each item in turn. I was in 'hog heaven.' I ate it all in one sitting."

Not long after her feast, Jean-Marie felt sicker than she'd ever felt in her life. When she went to find her mother, Eileen panicked. Her daughter looked worse than she'd ever seen her. Her daughter's eyes were glazed and her stomach distended. Eileen tried to lift Jean-Marie in her arms and her kidneys nearly ruptured. Ten minutes later, Jean-Marie was bouncing on a stretcher, as two GIs rushed her to the nearest emergency aid station.

"I was in a makeshift hospital room in the Education Building. When they put me on the bed, I looked up and noticed a huge hole in the ceiling above me. I asked what happened, and the doctor said that a shell had come through the roof, destroying the bed directly under it. After they cleaned up, they put a new bed in. The doctor told me, 'But don't worry, kiddo, lightning doesn't strike twice in the same spot.' Somehow, I didn't find that very reassuring."

Eileen held Jean-Marie's hand, while her daughter moaned in pain. For the first time that morning, she had time to notice that Jean-Marie's skin was an incredibly bright, lemon yellow. The whites of her eyes were tinted the same poisoned shade. The doctor made an immediate diagnosis. This certainly wasn't the first internee with food poisoning, and certainly wouldn't be the last. He pumped Jean-Marie's stomach and hooked her up to an intravenous tube, prescribing a glucose diet for the indefinite future. Since his arrival at Santo Tomas, he had done the same for at least fifty internees. He had broadcast his message over the loudspeaker and had posted it in the halls, "Be moderate! Food madness can be fatal!"

Jean-Marie was in the hospital for a week.

After waiting an hour, Eileen finally reached the front of the line. The army clerk, seated behind a card table, deigned to spare her a brief glance, before burying himself again in his forms.

"You are an American citizen?"

"Yes."

"Married?"

"Yes."

"Fill out three of these for every member of your family. Do you wish to be repatriated to the United States of America?"

"Yes."

"East or West?"

"Excuse me?"

An exasperated sigh. "Do you wish to go to the east or west coast of America? New York or San Francisco?"

"San Francisco."

"Are you willing to sign this statement promising to repay the American Red Cross for the cost of your passage?"

"Excuse me? You're kidding, right?"

"No ma'am. Do you or don't you wish to sign this statement promising... "

Gene interrupted, "Fine, we'll sign. But this is the biggest load of malarkey I've ever heard."

Gene and Eileen were outraged. They couldn't believe what they were hearing. Here they were, liberated prisoners of war, in failing health, not a penny to their names, no jobs, two children, and to get back to the States they would have to go into debt.

"Sign here, here, here and here. Thank you. Be ready to move out tomorrow morning at oh-seven hundred. Trucks leave from the main plaza."

"When?"

"Seven o'clock. Try to keep your baggage to a minimum."

Eileen laughed out loud. She was dressed in drab, Red Cross emergency clothing, and she still had wooden bakyas on her feet, which were too swollen with beriberi to fit into normal shoes. The clerk finally looked up from his forms. Internees in line behind Eileen had been grinning and shaking their heads, thinking of the extent of their own "baggage."

"Oh, I'll sure try," Eileen said, sarcastically. "But, gee-whiz, mister officer, sir. I've got so many pretty things to wear, whatever will I do?"

"That'll be enough of that! Don't you know there's a war on?"

Gene's hand shot out and grabbed a fistful of the corporal's shirt. After three years of bowing from the waist, the internees had put with as much bureaucratic arrogance as they could stand for several lifetimes to come.

"Listen to me, you little pip-squeak! You think we've come this far to be afraid of someone like you! Zero seven hundred! Minimum baggage! We'll be there!"

The clerk was about to put him in his place when he noticed the expressions of the internees in line behind the Faggiano's. He swallowed hard and sat down.

Eileen was putting the finishing stitches onto Jean-Marie's "Victory Apron." The final bit of embroidery read, "Liberated by U.S. Army, Feb.

3, 1945." Eileen was seated on the family's entire worldly possessions, all contained in one small bamboo suitcase.

Jean-Marie, Jimmy, and Gene sat cross-legged on the grass of the main plaza, surrounded by the other 360 internees due to leave that day. The army trucks had arrived an hour ago and seemed ready to board, but the internees had been asked to wait. They were growing used to this, as the army seemed to have their own sense of time. Anything colored khaki or painted olive drab invariably required a great deal of waiting.

Two armored personnel carriers, mounted with heavy machine guns, covered the front and rear of the convoy of five open trucks. Once the APC's were in place, each truck was filled to their maximum capacity with departing internees. For the first mile or so, the trucks, driving over rubble and wreckage, rolled slowly along, accompanied by a flanking escort of foot soldiers in the event of an ambush. As they reached the outskirts of the city, the infantry escort turned back. The column was formed and ready to go. Engines revved up and the trucks went back into gear.

Jean-Marie took a long last look at the mass of waving hands and smiling faces of well wishers in the camp. The main buildings had withstood the shell fire, wounded and scarred, but still the same solid, dreary, hulking shapes that had grown to be the backdrop of her whole world. Here, her father flew his kite on the day of the great kite fight. She saw the escape pipe that she and Jimmy, thankfully, never had to use. She saw the spot outside the kitchen where Bumblebee snuck rice cakes to her. She saw the cart that her father and Jack Cassidy used to haul food from the front gate to the bodega, now abandoned near a lone palm tree.

On the day of the liberation, 3,768 prisoners were inside the gates of Santo Tomas Internment Camp. During their confinement, seven prisoners had been executed. Over 450 prisoners had died of starvation and disease related illnesses. Adding the prisoners killed after the liberation from enemy action, the total death toll came to approximately 475 people.

The Faggiano's truck was the last in the column, and as it slowly rolled out the front gate, Jean-Marie stood up and grasped the top of the tailgate and deliberately fixed her last image of Santo Tomas in her mind. She watched the highest point in camp, the clock tower, recede in the distance.

Jean-Marie knew no matter how far she went, no matter how old a woman she would become, she would never forget.

Manila stank with a heavy, cloying, sweetish perfume of decay that lay in almost tangible swirls over the ruins, catching in the throats of the internees, settling on their clothes and hair, drifting with the smoke and dust and permeating the stagnant, humid atmosphere. Bloated, unburied corpses lay in clusters by the roadside, like knots of driftwood left stranded at high tide, torn and picked at by flocks of large black scavenger birds. Soldiers walked among the slowly rolling trucks of the convoy, giving out paper respirator masks.

Eileen pointed to a street sign that had somehow managed to stay unscathed by the devastation that surrounded it. Her voice muffled by the respirator, Eileen said, "Del Pilar Street. That's where our house was."

What had been a quiet, tree-lined, residential neighborhood, had been reduced to jagged dunes of smoldering, blackened rubble. Gone were the flowering vines, the rows of tulips, the bamboo groves, the palm trees, the milkman, the postman, the gardeners, the laughing brown schoolgirls with their long, black braids and their starched plaid, Catholic school dresses. Broken brick, splintered wood, twisted pipes, and mangled tree trunks were all that remained of their life before the war. Jean-Marie realized with a start that all the pictures from her past, the church on the corner, the Montinola girls, Anselma, Corky the springer spaniel, Hernando the cockatoo, her mother's rose garden, the bomb shelter, garden parties with tiny, magical Japanese umbrellas peeking from the top of iced cocktail glasses -- all these things and countless others -- now existed solely as a memory in her own mind.

The GI was hot and tired, his feet were sweaty and blistered, and the pack straps were cutting off his circulation at his shoulders, killing all sensation in his hands. A Browning automatic lay across his shoulders, thirty-eight pounds of pure misery. His face suddenly lit up as he realized the solution to his problems had been right under his nose for the past two hours. He quickened his pace and caught up with the tailgate of the last truck.

"Have you guys got room for my stuff in there?"

"Sure! Throw it in!"

The bed of the truck was crowded, but the internees pulled in their legs to make room for the soldier's backpack. They could sympathize, knowing that none of them could even have lifted the huge pack, bristling with lethal equipment. The soldier threw off his burden and heaved it into the truck. His three partners smiled in admiration, suffering under the combined weight of their packs, steel helmets, rifles, and several heavy boxes of spare ammo. They were positioned too far back from the trucks for their buddy's brilliant plan to work for them. Officers would notice and investigate. The lead man was shielded from sight by the back of the last truck. He slung his carbine on top of the pack, keeping the big Browning automatic across his shoulders. He felt a thousand pounds lighter. Life was wonderful.

"Thank you! That pack was killing me! Hey, where you guys going?"

"You mean you don't know?"

The GI grinned, pulled off his helmet and wiped the dripping sweat from his face.

"Hey, I'm just a private. They don't tell me diddly!"

He was in his early twenties, blond and blue-eyed, with a pug nose and a polite, Midwestern twang. He might as well have been wearing a tag that said "Farmer's Son."

"Where are you from, soldier?"

"Iowa, little place near Davenport..."

The soldier spotted the pretty little girl with the blonde curls, sitting nearby.

"Hey, little girl, where are you from?"

"I was born in Shanghai, China."

The young soldier looked at Jean-Marie with a puzzled expression on his face.

"China? Well, I'll be darned..."

He studied her face closely.

"You sure about that? 'Cause you sure don't *look* Chinese."

The truckload of internees giggled at first, then began laughing out loud. Jean-Marie laughed until she had tears coming out of her eyes. The young man finally caught on and joined the rest in hearty laughter.

It felt good to laugh again.

Late in the afternoon they came to the end of the road. Three hundred and sixty five internees piled out of the trucks and looked around in puzzled confusion. They were in the countryside north of Manila, at the edge of a dense jungle, essentially in the middle of nowhere.

"The soldiers told us to follow them and stay close. Someone asked how far we had to go, and they told us that we had about an hour's walk ahead of us."

Jimmy spotted it first... a crippled Japanese fighter plane lying in the depths of the jungle, not far from the path. The Zero was festooned with lush, purple bougainvillea vines.

The internees stepped from the dripping depths of a cool rain forest, where it was impossible to see a yard ahead, out onto a perfectly level, prefabricated airfield. The internees and GIs collapsed in the shade by the side of the air strip, their last reserves of energy burnt up by the trek through the jungle. Both Gene and Jimmy were running high fevers and barely had the strength to stand.

"Our plane finally arrived, and I was so excited because I had never been in an airplane before. And the best part was that I had a window seat! I was so excited, I could barely sit still. The plane began rolling down the runway, and I was awestruck. First the thunder of the engines, then the race down the runway while the power of the airplane rumbled louder, then the sudden lift, and the ground fading far away!"

The plane leaned over and circled the field, gaining altitude by the second. Another C-47, rolling to a stop on the ground below, looked like a toy. Clean, cool air rushed from the vents over their heads. It was a majestic, noble, marvelous feeling to soar above the world, leaving the heat and stench below.

Jean-Marie could see beyond the jungle, out onto the earth's horizon, all the way to Manila. The site of the distant city was marked by huge hanging canopies of drowsy smoke. The C-47 moved up into the clouds and for a while, and Jean-Marie stared into a sea of gray nothingness. Then, with amazing speed, the plane burst into the dazzling realm of sunlight, above the clouds, stretching into a glorious sea of shining, brilliant blue. It was wonderful, miraculous. All the fear and pain were hidden somewhere under the endless ocean of beautiful white clouds.

Jean-Marie was mesmerized by the beauty of the clouds when she suddenly spotted some more airplanes. She tapped her father on the shoulder and pointed at the planes. Gene leaned over and glanced out the port.

"Good deal! A fighter escort! These guys are really on the beam!"

Jean-Marie gasped as her feet suddenly left the floor and she seemed to float off her seat. The C-47 slid into an almost perpendicular, screaming nosedive, howling toward the ground like a torpedo. Twenty-two internees screamed bloody murder. For another hour the plane would stay deep in the clouds, ducking and diving, as internee faces turned green with motion sickness.

They landed in the middle of a heavy monsoon storm. Huddling docilely together, the small group waited for transport, sheltered from the torrential rain under the wings of the aircraft. Night was falling and they still had no notion where they were. A jeep without headlights pulled up from out of the gloom, honking its horn for the pilot and co-pilot. The two young flyers emerged from the cockpit and climbed down under the wing, politely making their way through the crowd of internees.

Gene spotted the two pilots and worked his way up to them.

"Dad was angry. He said, 'Hey, what was that roller coaster ride all about? We're all sick as hell! You guys had an escort!' The pilots looked at him, and one of them said, 'Sir, those weren't escorts. Those were Jap Zeros.' Dad couldn't believe it. He asked them why they didn't use their guns, and they told him that the C-47s weren't equipped with them."

The skillful pilots had used the cloud cover to evade the Japanese fighter planes. Somehow, miraculously, it worked.

"We found out that we were in Leyte, near Tacloban. They told us that there was a big evacuation port just beyond the trees, and that it was all downhill from this point on."

A truck dropped the exhausted and bedraggled internees off in front of an enormous tent that was, due to unforeseen meteorological circumstances, waist deep in water. As they watched, several of their assigned bunks floated out of the entrance of the tent and drifted toward the ocean.

After more hours of inquiry and being sent from one functionary to another, the weary travelers eventually found a warm welcome, spending the night on the dry, wooden floor of the Red Cross canteen. Jean-Marie woke up with the sun. Before any of the other internees were stirring, she tip-toed out of the canteen, quietly closing the spring-hinged screen door behind her.

She turned toward the ocean and gasped in wonder; it was staggering, infinite, and awash with glowing, jewel-like colors. In this new world there were no walls. The gently surging ocean was huge, endless.

Jean-Marie let her eyes roam the vast horizon, far out where the sunrise was just breaking in a delicate saffron glow. Never again would she willingly let herself be confined. A warm, tangy salt breeze blew in from the sea.

Jean-Marie filled her lungs with the fragrant air and smiled.

Chapter Ten

March 1945

The evacuation center consisted of a huge, improvised seaport, teeming with liberty ships and merchant marine vessels, landing craft, ammo ships, hospital ships, and oil tankers. All of these vessels were being loaded and unloaded on what had been, not six months before, a deserted stretch of scenic beach. Ten thousand men lived in tents at the edge of the jungle.

Before the first marine jumped into the Tacloban surf, naval gunfire had spent several hours moving the tree line half a mile back from the beach. Now the flattened space between the beach and the trees was filled to overflowing.

Jean-Marie marveled at the size of the encampment. The entire population of Santo Tomas would be swallowed up in an ocean of barracks, Quonset huts, and endless rows of one man pup tents and vast clusters of large mess tents. Cargo ships lined the horizon and the surf was thick with streams of amphibious vehicles and landing craft. Formations of Marine Corsair fighters patrolled the air overhead.

"I was completely ready to forgo the trip to America. Aside from the fact that my arms were rigid with inoculations for every disease known to man, I was having a wonderful time. There was food and more food, swimming in the ocean, movies every night, and thousands of American soldiers to talk to. I would have been perfectly content to spend the rest of my life on Tacloban beach, where I was every soldier's pampered kid sister."

Early in the morning, Eileen had made sandwiches and lemonade for her two children and sent them on a beach walk. Over the last few days, Jean-Marie and Jimmy had made friends with one of the young GIs who took them in as their "Big Brother." He was the first adult to understand that they really weren't children anymore, chronological time notwithstanding. He took them seriously as liberated POWs and treated them as equals.

While the three of them were walking along the beach, Jean-Marie accidently stepped on something near the water that made her jump backwards with a gasp. Jean-Marie and Jimmy stared at the slimy lump in the sand.

"At first we thought it might have been a jellyfish. Then our GI friend leaned over, took a closer look, and said, 'That's no jellyfish. That's somebody's stomach.'

"Sure enough, on closer examination the gray white object seemed to have more tubes and valves than a jellyfish ought to. I wondered out loud if it was a Japanese stomach or an American stomach, and the GI said there was no way to find out. He said we should bury it, though, because it didn't matter now which side he was on."

Jean-Marie and her brother tied two branches together to form a cross. They dug a slit in the sand with their hands, burying the stomach at the edge of a peaceful palm grove with a sweeping ocean view. The GI said the service.

"Oh, Lord, accept the poor dead man who owned this stomach into your grace. He was just a soldier, and he did what he had to do, so please have mercy on his soul. Amen."

"Amen."

The Faggiano's were seated at the outdoor theater that night, watching Jimmy Cagney in "The Public Enemy." At the moment when the young thug was snarling his immortal "I wish you was a wishing well!" a GI sitting several rows ahead of Gene slumped forward, bending from the waist onto his knees. A half hour later, during Cagney's ruthless rise to the top of the Chicago mob, someone noticed that the soldier hadn't moved in all that time. People around him began to worry, and when someone tapped him on the arm, the Marine fell out of his seat and onto the ground. His chest was covered with blood, brains, and bone splinters. The back of his head had been shot off. Minutes later, powerful searchlights converged on the splintered, ragged top of a tall palm tree, the highest point left in the charred debris of the forest overlooking the beach. Three submachine guns chewed the fronds to fragments, and seconds later an emaciated figure fell to the ground, riddled with bullet holes.

A Marine intelligence officer examined the ragged, lice-ridden corpse and recoiled in stunned amazement, realizing that this man's unit had been cleared off the beach months before. Where had he hidden? How had he survived? How many thousands of American troops had marched under his tree?

Chapter Eleven

April 1945

Jean-Marie shielded her eyes against the early morning glare that bounced off the rolling green surface of the sea.

"Is that the boat to San Francisco?"

"No, sweetie. That boat's going to take us out to the big ship! It's one of those big ones, out there." Eileen pointed to the horizon where a procession of squat gray shapes wallowed under the shadow of a dark squall.

"I asked my father what the difference was between a boat and a ship. He smiled and told me, 'Honey, boats are small and ships are big. You can put a boat on a ship, but you can't put a ship on a boat!'"

Jean-Marie looked up at the sheer gray sides of the troop ship, the Admiral Capps, towering above her. The soldier already had one foot on the landing net and was coaxing her to climb onto his back and hold on to his neck. Behind her, a line of internees and wounded soldiers struggled to maintain their balance on the slippery steel deck of the landing craft. Rough seas drenched the passengers in showers of spray, keeping them hanging onto handholds, striving to keep their belongings from rolling and sloshing through puddles of water across the bottom of the empty landing craft.

"I really didn't know how much of a fear of heights I had until that day, when we boarded the Admiral Capps. I was scared to death! I finally gathered up my courage and wrapped my arms around the neck of the GI. I closed my eyes and didn't open them again until we were half way up the net. One swift glance was enough. We were dangling stories from the surface of the sea, and the rough waters were making the boat smash against the side of the Admiral Capps. I knew if we fell into that space of water between the ship and the boat, it was going to be all over. I shut my eyes again and with all the strength in my toothpick arms, I held on to that soldier's neck as tightly as I possibly could."

By sunset, the Admiral Capps was fifty miles from Leyte, steaming in convoy with a sister ship some miles to the right and two frigates covering the point and the rear. The ship was crammed to its limits with wounded or furloughed soldiers, Filipino refugees, liberated internees, and POWs. As the sun touched the horizon, the crew breathed a sigh of relief and leaned back from their guns. In a few moments, darkness would fall and by morning they would have left the danger zone far behind. Men stretched, took off their helmets, glanced at their wrist watches, thought about dinner, and about all the cute, liberated nurses on board.

The next morning, three huge, black, floating balls of explosives, bristling with magnetic contact points, were spotted by the forward watch in the nick of time. The convoy made a wide detour around the mines, then, as the last frigate was safely out of range, they took out the spherical sea monsters with their guns, using them for target practice.

The sailors had given some thought to the children who were to be their passengers, constructing a large sandbox made from Leyte beach sand, complete with swings and a set of monkey bars. There was a game room for checkers and Parcheesi, and a canteen for Hershey bars and chocolate milk.

Jean-Marie and Jimmy quickly adjusted to life onboard the Admiral Capps. They pointed at the schools of flying fish, fought over who was going to get the top bunk on the six tier bunk beds, and giggled over their meals that had a habit of sliding out from under their spoons and forks to go crashing into the ridges bolted to the edge of the mess table. While Gene and Eileen spent hours a day asleep in their bunks, emerging chiefly for meals, Jean-Marie and Jimmy explored every exciting inch of the ship, barring the areas from which civilians were restricted. Aside from a traumatic visit to the ship's dentist, Jean-Marie found life aboard the ship even more fun than she could've imagined. "Belay that!" "Now hear this!" "Lay down to the mess deck!" "The smoking lamp is out!" She loved the weird language of sailors.

The weather was getting colder daily, and the passengers were issued woolen, Navy-blue pea coats. With her hands snuggled down into the pockets of her pea coat and her sailor's cap slung low over her eyes, Jean-Marie felt like one of the crew, watching the ocean spray fly across the deck. She knew her father was going to try and get his old job back with

American President Lines. Maybe she could sail with him and be his helper and spend her life at sea, with no boundaries, no worries, just the waves rolling to the horizon.

Jean-Marie was playing checkers one afternoon with an army major. She had just beaten him for the third time.

"I kept winning at checkers, and he laughed and said I was pretty good. I explained that I spent many monsoon afternoons playing the game back in Santo Tomas, so I had a lot of practice. He offered to reward me for beating him so consistently, since he claimed he was a pretty good checkers player himself and didn't get beat often. He offered to take me to the mess deck for a pop or a candy bar, but I told him that was okay, he didn't have to do that."

The major noticed, however, that Jean-Marie was preoccupied with his exotic brass insignia. She asked him what they were, and he told her they were oak leaf clusters, signifying that he was a major in the army. He smiled and removed the oak leafs from his shoulders and gestured for Jean-Marie to lean across the table, where he pinned his brass onto her dress. He grinned and said, "There you go!" and gave her a salute. Jean-Marie was beaming, and even got a rush of pleasure as she pictured her brother shriveling with envy. She looked back at the major and, after sitting up as straight as possible, she returned his salute.

"I offered to play another game of checkers with him, but he declined and jokingly said that he couldn't take another beating from me. Then he got serious for a moment and leaned across the table. He looked me in the eye and said, 'You know something? You're a very fortunate young lady. You're really special. Listen, when you get back to the States, for the first little while you're going to be, well, different than the other kids. They might not believe you when you tell them were you've been. But I want you to remember something. Never be ashamed of yourself, if they don't understand you. You hear me? You've already seen more, done more, and been through more, than they could ever dream of.'"

Jean-Marie was sure there were innumerable sins she had committed in the time of her internment, but there was only one absolutely unforgivable crime that stood out prominently.

"Forgive me father for I have sinned."

"What was the nature of the sin my child?"

"Well..."

Jean-Marie wasn't sure what might happen. After all, one didn't swipe the body of Christ.

"You know the host... the wafers in church?"

"Yes, go on."

"One day... um, I sneaked into the tent chapel and ate a whole bunch of them. And after that, there were no more for the priests... or... um, anyone, actually... because I ate every last one of them."

"Is that all?" He tried to keep the smile out of his voice.

"Yes, Father."

"Were you very hungry my child?"

"Yes, Father."

"Do you think that God knew you were hungry?"

"I suppose. Yes, He probably did, Father."

"You are forgiven, my dear. Say three Hail Mary's and go in peace."

Jean-Marie stood on the deck at the bow of the Admiral Capps and shivered with the wind. It was the coldest wind that ever raised goose flesh up and down her legs. She couldn't stop trembling, no matter how many layers of clothes Eileen piled on her. That morning, every passenger had been sprayed with DDT. Even with the heavy wind and fog, the entire ship stank of it.

"We were closing in on San Francisco Bay, and I was so excited. America was looming right before our eyes. The site of the San Francisco skyline was absolutely breathtaking.

"As soon as the Admiral Capps got closer to the Golden Gate Bridge, I looked at Dad and asked him, 'Why is it orange? I though you said it was supposed to be golden?' He laughed and said, 'It's orange? Well, I'll be damned. Heck, I didn't know that, either.' And he didn't. My dad was colorblind."

The deck was jammed with crying, cheering people. Pilot boats were already in place, leading the Admiral Capps through the perilous "potato patch" at the mouth of the harbor. Jean-Marie stared up at the colossus of the Golden Gate as the ship, dwarfed by the vaulting, soaring angles of the fantastic structure, slid underneath its arch and into the blue waters of San Francisco Bay.

Fire ships were saluting the Admiral Capps with fountains of spray. From all over the harbor, whistles blasted. The Admiral Capps answered, deafening the passengers. On the piers of Fort Mason, a happy, celebrating crowd had gathered under a huge "WELCOME HOME" banner. Sea gulls swept over the water. A brass band was playing.

The Faggiano's went through the last formalities, standing on the various customs and Red Cross lines that stretched down the length of a vast, drafty, hanger-like building. Army nurses led Jean-Marie and Jimmy away to the children's area for milk and cookies, after a dozen multicolored entry tags had been safety pinned to their pea coats.

Jimmy looked over the crowd of waving relatives, waiting behind a military police barrier a hundred feet away.

"Where are Grandpa and Grandma? Is Aunt Consie there, Mom? Can you see any of them, Dad?"

There were numerous relatives waiting nearby, a sea of jubilant faces.

"I was so cold. I was so used to the tropical climates, and this new place seemed like the North Pole to me!"

Suddenly a voice rang out.

"Gene! Eileen! Kids! Over here!"

It was Gene's sister, Constance, or Consie as she was called, leading the way toward them. Right behind her were Gene's parents. Several ecstatic moments followed as the family members hugged and kissed.

Aunt Consie stood back and looked at her nephew and niece. "Jean-Marie, my dear, this is the first time I've ever laid eyes on you! My goodness, you're going to be a heartbreaker! And Jimmy, what a handsome lad you're turning into! Gene and Eileen, why don't you two ride back to San Rafael with Mom and Dad, and I'll drive the kids. We've got a meal waiting for all of you at home that's going to knock your socks off!"

Constance Faggiano was a tall woman and tough as nails. Not as Jean-Marie imagined her, but her own person. She had an air of courage and self-sufficiency. She could take care of herself.

"Where do you want to ride, honey?"

"Can I ride up there under the window in the back?"

"Sure! You'll get a good look at the bay from there!"

Jean-Marie climbed up into the space beneath the rear window and watched America, spring of 1945, roll by. She took in the strange pine and eucalyptus trees of the Presidio, the choppy water of the bay, topped by whitecaps, the sweep of the bridge, the clean pastel feeling of the San Francisco streets and hills.

She was half way to San Rafael before she remembered.

She was finally going to see the ice cream store!

That dream of eating all the ice cream she could possibly eat in Grandma's store was the dream that kept her going during some of the toughest times in Santo Tomas. And now, maybe even today, she was going to see it for the first time and splurge on a sundae, covered with chocolate syrup and maybe even a cherry on top! Her mouth began to water with the thought.

"Aunt Consie, before we go home, can we stop by Grandma's ice cream shop? Please, please, please?"

Constance Faggiano laughed, stubbed out her cigarette in the ashtray and changed into third, giving the blue '41 Ford sedan extra gas for the steep Waldo Grade ahead.

"Funny you should mention that, sweetheart. The State's building a highway right through the middle of town. Your grandmother had to sell the place about two weeks ago."

Chapter Twelve

July 1964

With her husband and children already in bed, Jean-Marie returned to the dining room. She sat down at the large dining room table where she had spent most of the afternoon and evening telling her two eldest sons the story of Santo Tomas. The boys had been mesmerized by the story, and even after Jean-Marie had finished telling it, the boys had a million questions to ask. It was obvious, too, that they had developed a new respect for their mother, their uncle Jimmy, and their grandparents.

Jean-Marie looked at the doll lying on the table. She thought of Private Tanner, the soldier who gave her the doll, and smiled when she remembered the way in which he coaxed her to take it from him. She wondered if he made it back home again to Frederick, Oklahoma. She vowed to try and contact him and his family soon, to see if he'd remember her and to thank him again.

Jean-Marie closed her eyes for a moment, and in the silence of the room she thought she could hear the distant sound of anti-aircraft guns firing. She knew it was just her imagination, aided by the sound of the wind blowing through the trees outside. Her imagination would sometimes follow her into her sleep as well. There were the nightmares, yes, but she also had the good memories. She saw her father, mother, and Jimmy, singing "Happy Birthday" to her with a fake candle sticking out of a mound of rice mush. She thought of Bumblebee and his smile and unbreakable spirit. She thought of Mrs. Boycott and the "Recipe Game," Moira Malone and her movie actress looks, and the first crush she ever had on a boy who gave her a broken lens and a piece of leather as a gift. She let her thoughts go back to the days on Del Pilar, playing with the Montinola children, with Hansel and Gretel yapping at her heels.

She also remembered the Japanese soldiers that gave the internee children piggy-back rides, and the one young soldier that called her "Shelly Temple" and gave her the candy-coated almonds.

Jean-Marie was suddenly filled with emotion, and tears began to fill her eyes. In her thirty-seven months as a prisoner of war, she had experienced the absolute worst in human suffering and brutality, but she had also experienced the absolute best in human courage, love, and faith. She said a silent prayer, thanking God for her life and for those brought to her life. She lived in a beautiful home on a farm in the country with a happy, healthy family that loved her as much as she loved them. And because of the sacrifices of many brave souls, she was given this gift of precious freedom, to savor and enjoy for the rest of her years.

She reached down and picked up the doll, and, after holding it tenderly in her hands for several contemplative moments, gently put it back inside the wooden box.

Epilogue

After the Faggiano family returned to the United States, they made their home in San Rafael, California, not far from Gene's mother's house. Gene got his job back with American President Lines and Eileen enjoyed gardening and playing Mahjong with her friends. Jimmy and Jean-Marie went to elementary school at St. Anselm's Catholic School in San Anselmo, and secondary school at Marin Catholic High School in Kentfield.

Jimmy entered the U. S. Air Force after high school, and grew up to be as handsome a man as his father. Jimmy married, had children, and followed his lifelong love of animals by becoming a trainer of police dogs. To this day, he is one of the most respected trainers of dogs for K-9 units. Jimmy owns his own business and lives in Pleasanton, California.

Gene reunited with his old friend, Jack Cassidy, and true to their vow to celebrate with a party at the St. Francis in San Francisco once they made it back to the States, they did just that. It was a glorious night, and Gene wore a white dinner jacket, just like the one he used to wear when he took Eileen out to dinner at the Manila Hotel before the war. As Gene and Eileen headed out the door to drive to San Francisco, Jean-Marie had a bout of déjà vu, remembering the day in the prison camp when she saw her father at his worst. Now, he looked like a movie star again, trim and fit and healthy. Her mother was equally stunning, clad in a beautiful evening gown with shimmering jewelry. Jean-Marie smiled and waved at her parents as they drove away. She remembered how bad things had gotten for them, and how they both almost didn't survive. She remembered all of the silent prayers that she said every night in the prison camp, asking God to watch over them. As she stood on the porch and watched their car turn the corner, she gently caressed the gold cross that hung at the end of her necklace.

At the St. Francis that night, the Cassidy's and the Faggiano's toasted to their friendship. It was a night of laughter, celebration, and plenty of memories. Jack's time in Los Banos had been tough on him, and more than a few times he felt that he wasn't going to make it. He told Gene, though, that he knew he had a promise to keep with his good friend. And he was a man of his word.

That night at the St. Francis turned into a celebration of friendship that continued for many years, as the Faggiano's and the Cassidy's remained lifelong friends.

Gene and Eileen enjoyed many years together and both lived long and fruitful lives. They loved spending time with their grandchildren. Gene used to take the grandkids out to Stinson beach and show them how to fly kites. Just like the internees at Santo Tomas, the children were fascinated by his kite flying expertise. Eileen used to spoil the grandchildren with candy and treats every time they'd visit. Still the tough woman that she was in the prison camp days, she gave stern warnings to the children on how they should never leave a plate of food half-eaten. A meal at the Faggiano household was a big event, and a prayer of gratitude was always given before each meal. Some things aren't easily forgotten.

Ken Kitagawa was seventeen years old and had only a modest understanding of the family in the United States that would be his host over the summer of 1973. He didn't care, though. They seemed like a nice family from all he had read in the exchange student program papers, and he was excited to be spending that summer in California on a little farm in Sonoma, just north of San Francisco. Ken had lived in Japan all his life, and the thought of being in America as an exchange student was literally a dream come true for him.

Ken spent that summer living with a remarkable family, and with an even more remarkable host mother. She actually knew some Japanese and, albeit a bit rusty, could hold a conversation with him in his native tongue. She seemed to understand him better than most of the Americans he had met in his short time in the United States. She seemed to possess the wisdom of a woman much older in years. There was a certain knowledge behind her green eyes.

That summer she took him to Disneyland, to the county fair, to San Francisco, to everywhere. He never had so much fun, and his visit to America was the experience of his life.

At the end of summer, on the day he was to leave for home, the host family said their tearful goodbyes. The mother of the family drove him to the San Francisco International Airport for his return trip to Tokyo. As she escorted him to the gate, she handed him a wrapped gift, saying, "This is for you, Ken. Have a safe journey, and I will miss you very much." They hugged tightly, both with tears in their eyes.

Later, as the plane traveled across the Pacific, Ken Kitagawa opened his gift.

It was a box, filled with candy-coated almonds.

Ken would never know that this was exactly the same kind of candy that a young Japanese soldier, on the eve of his fateful trip to Bataan many years ago, would give to a little girl in Santo Tomas that he fondly referred to as "Shelly Temple." It was an act of kindness that she never forgot.

Ken put a candy into his mouth and savored the wonderful taste, watching the wisps of clouds outside his window floating free and easy over the vast expanse of the endless blue Pacific below.

In October of 1975, Jean-Marie decided to contact the soldier that gave her the Japanese doll during the liberation. From the article and picture in "Stars and Stripes" magazine, she knew his name was Theo Tanner and that he was from Frederick, Oklahoma. She called directory assistance and, after getting a series of wrong numbers with a few Theodore Tanner's, she finally got through to the correct Tanner household, living in Lawton, Oklahoma. She never knew that his real name was just Theo; she thought that Theo was just an abbreviation for Theodore.

A warm and friendly voice answered the phone. Theo's wife, Ullainee, listened carefully as Jean-Marie explained who she was and how she knew Theo. There was silence on the other end of the phone for a beat, and then Ullainee began to speak. Her voice quivered with emotion. She said softly, "My God... he always spoke of you. He remembered you and always wondered how you were." Jean-Marie had trouble finding her own voice. "Is he... is Theo home? May I say hello? I wanted to... thank him again... " More silence on the phone, and Ullainee finally spoke in an unsteady voice. "No, my dear... Theo passed away a few years ago. I'm... I'm so sorry... Theo would've been so happy to have heard from you." Ullainee took a deep breath. "We still have the picture on the hearth, of the two of you together, with Theo giving you that doll. It was the only memory of the war that gave him peace and happiness."

And at that, Jean-Marie and Ullainee Tanner wept together.

On March 4, 2008, Jean-Marie, along with her son, Michael, her daughter-in-law Angela, and Jean-Marie's good friend, Elvira Magsambol, made a trip to the Philippines to visit Manila. It had been sixty-three years since she left the University of Santo Tomas, and now she wanted to return.

This time, voluntarily.

Months prior to her departure to the Philippines, Jean-Marie got an email from her son, Michael, informing her that he had found the Montinola family web site. Through the web site, Jean-Marie sent an email explaining who she was and how she and her family had lived with the Montinola family many years ago. One of the sons of Aurelio Sr., Sergio Montinola, wrote back to Jean-Marie and expressed his utter happiness and joy to hear from her again after all of these years. Sergio and Jean-Marie exchanged several emails to each other, and soon a trip to the Philippines went from an idea to a reality.

"Going back to the Philippines was actually a lifelong dream of mine. I have always wanted to go back and visit, especially accompanied by members of my family.

"When Michael and I began planning our trip, he asked me if I was at all nervous about going back to Santo Tomas. I replied that I didn't feel any nervousness about it, but the day we stepped off of the airplane in Manila, I felt this chill go up my spine. It was a brief sensation of fear, and as quickly, it passed. When the day finally came that we went to Santo Tomas for our visit, I was actually feeling excited about going and seeing it again. As we drove down the Calle Espana, I didn't recognize the university at first. My God, it had changed so much over the years. I expected it to, but the memory of the camp that I had etched in my brain for all of these years didn't match the scene before me. The campus was filled with young, healthy students, who were busy taking their classes at what is today one of the major universities in the Philippines. The campus was beautiful.

"As we drove from the entrance towards the center of the campus, I spotted the Main Building. There it was, with the clock tower and everything, looking almost exactly as it looked back when I saw it last, in 1945.

"After we parked the van, Michael, Angela, Elvira, Sergio, and I all walked up to the Main Building entrance. I stood there for a moment and was doing fine, until Michael asked me, with his video camera rolling, how it felt to be here again. And suddenly I felt the tears well up in my eyes. I couldn't find the words to describe what I was feeling just then. I was overwhelmed, to say the least.

"I walked up to the building and put my hand on the cool surface of the facade. Looking upwards I could see the window on the second floor where my mother and I used to live, in Room 48. The front of the building still carries the marks and scars of the artillery and gunfire from the war."

Jean-Marie, Michael, Angela, and Elvira spent two days touring the University of Santo Tomas. On the first day, Jean-Marie led the tour, stopping and describing the events that she remembered happening in certain parts of the building, both inside and outside. On that tour of the Main Building, they met with Maita Oebanda, curator for the university museum. Maita graciously gave the group a complete tour of the campus the following day.

Like the Main Building, the Education Building still exists today, but with some modern additions made to the front of the building. The Gymnasium and the Seminary buildings are still there, but the Annex is gone. Jean-Marie marveled at the large secondary school that had been built on the campus, and the large green sports field that is near the area where Dave Harvey used to have his stage show set up. Not far from where the "Little Theater Under the Stars" used to be, students were now busily involved in an enthusiastic game of soccer.

"I think the one thing I felt the best about from revisiting Santo Tomas was the fact that today it is filled with such happiness and hope. When the University was a prison camp, these were the two things that many of us didn't have a lot of. It gladdens my heart today to see how Santo Tomas has become such a positive place for these young men and women."

Michael and Angela McCoy returned home after a week in Manila, while Jean-Marie and her friend Elvira spent another two weeks in the

Philippines, traveling to many cities, including Elvira's home in Cavite. They spent time in Intramuros and Tagaytay, and even took a guided tour of the island of Corregidor. During the Corregidor tour, the bus tour guide found out who Jean-Marie was and asked her if she wouldn't mind relating her experience as a POW to the tour group. After Jean-Marie spent a few moments speaking to the tourists, they approached her, one by one, and wanted to shake her hand. Jean-Marie smiled at them humbly and said, "Thank you, but I wouldn't be here today if it wasn't for the courage of men like those who fought on this island. They are the heroes. They should never be forgotten."

During Jean-Marie's visit to the Philippines, Sergio Montinola arranged a visit for Jean-Marie to meet with his sisters, the Montinola girls that signed her prayer book for her First Communion. Lourdes (Lulu) had passed away, but Jean-Marie was able to visit with Alice and Teresita. When the sisters saw the old prayer book that Jean-Marie brought with her, they smiled with the memory.

Sergio Montinola went out of his way to make the visit for Jean-Marie and her family memorable and pleasant. They visited the Malate church, just down the street from where the old house on Del Pilar used to be. Sergio then invited Jean-Marie and her family to meet his family living in Makati in the metropolitan area of Manila. Ching Montinola, the wife of Sergio and former presidential assistant for special projects with past presidents Corazon Aquino and Fidel Ramos, gave Jean-Marie and Elvira a special tour of the Philippine Presidential Palace.

"On the last week of our visit to the Philippines, we spent Easter Sunday at a gorgeous church in Cavite. It was the most beautiful service I have ever seen, and a fitting end to our trip. Elvira and I returned to the United States two days later, on March 25th.

"As we said our goodbyes to the Montinola family, I promised the Montinola's that, like Douglas MacArthur once famously said, 'I shall return.'"

Acknowledgements

This book could not have been published without the assistance and encouragement of many individuals to whom I would like to extend my most sincere gratitude.

Sergio Montinola was our gracious host during our stay in the Philippines, and was instrumental in making our trip the incredible and memorable experience that it was. We owe Sergio many thanks for his time and generosity, and we look forward to seeing him and his wonderful family again soon. A special thanks, too, to Ching Montinola, the wife of Sergio, for her graciousness and hospitality, and for giving Mom and Elvira the Presidential Palace tour. The Montinola family -- just like they were when my grandparents, uncle, and mother lived with them before the war -- were the nicest and most generous people you could ever meet.

I would like to extend a warm thank you to the "Montinola girls," Alice, Carmen, Teresita, and their families. It was a pleasure to meet you, and may we enjoy many years of friendship together. It meant the world to Mom to reunite with you after all of these years.

Maita Oebanda deserves special thanks. Maita is a collection management and documentation assistant at the University of Santo Tomas, as well as curator of the Museum of Arts and Sciences inside the Main Building. Maita was our tireless tour guide, and an incredible source of information regarding the history of the Japanese occupation of the Philippines during the war, and the extraordinary history of the University of Santo Tomas. Thank you, Maita!

To our close friend Elvira Magsambol, I offer my sincerest gratitude for coming with us on our trip to the Philippines and for the invaluable assistance you gave us all during our stay. We treasure your friendship and look forward to our next trip together.

I would like to acknowledge and thank Catharine Giordano and the staff at "Stars and Stripes" magazine for their extra efforts in helping with my research. Thank you for going above and beyond with your assistance, and for permission to use the photo of Jean-Marie with Private Tanner.

A heartfelt thanks to our book publisher, Strategic Book Publishing, for believing in us and making this dream come true. Thank you for your creativity, dedication, hard work, and professionalism.

To my grandparents, Eugene and Eileen Faggiano, I will always cherish my memories of you. Grandpa, I'm sure the angels are just as amazed as we were by your kite flying expertise. And Grandma, thank you for all of the years of love you bestowed upon all of us. I'll never forget your love, generosity, and strength of character.

To my uncle, James Faggiano, a special thanks for your warmth and humor over the years. I'm proud to be your nephew.

To my son, Tom, thank you for all of your enthusiasm, encouragement, and support during the making of this book. It has meant the world to me. I love you, son.

To my wonderful wife, Angela, thank you for sharing my passion for the completion of this book and for giving me the support I needed to spend countless hours in front of my computer, typing away day and night. I love you, Ang.

To the men and women who gave their lives during World War II -- from Europe to the Pacific -- may we never forget the sacrifice you made for us. For the soldiers of the First Cavalry, who led the liberation of Santo Tomas, I can't say enough. We owe you everything.

To the men and women of our armed forces who wear the uniform today, including my niece, Nicole Heskett, who is enlisted in the U.S. Air Force; I thank you for your service. You are appreciated deeply. I salute you.

I would like to also acknowledge the following individuals for their love and support in the making of this book: Tim Heskett, Shannon Zito, Kathleen Heskett, Jack Heskett, and Patrick Heskett; my brothers and sisters. Many thanks to you and your wonderful families... I love you all. A special acknowledgement to Bob and Lou Thompson, Mary and Gary Martin, Michele Miller, Justin and McCall Miller, Christine Downing (her father, Donald, was a POW in Los Banos), and to all of our many friends and family who have offered their kind support and love.

And finally, all of my love and thanks to that little girl with the "Shirley Temple" hair, who told me this story when I was a young boy. I'm so proud of you, Mom.

I know the ice cream store was gone when you got back to the States, but I know of another one, just downtown, that makes the best sundaes around.

My treat.

Bibliography

Cogan, Frances B. *Captured: The Japanese Internment of American Civilians in the Philippines, 1941 - 1945*. Athens GA: University of Georgia Press, 2000.

Connaughton, Pimlott, Anderson *The Battle for Manila*. Novato, CA: Presidio Press, 1995.

Holland, Robert *The Rescue of Santo Tomas*. Paducah, KY: Turner Publishing, 2003.

Labrador, O.P., Juan *A Diary of the Japanese Occupation*. Manila, Philippines: Santo Tomas University Press, 2000.

McCall, James E. *Santo Tomas Internment Camp: STIC in Verse and Reverse; STIC-toons and STIC-tistics*. Lincoln NE: Woodruff Printing Co., 1945.

Wetmore, Clio Matthews *Beyond Pearl Harbor*. Haverford, PA: Infinity Publishing, 2001.

The Author and His Mother

Michael McCoy

Michael is the eldest son of Jean-Marie Heskett (Faggiano). From the first time he heard the story of the internment of his mother, uncle, and grandparents in the Santo Tomas Internment Camp, he became fascinated with history, especially as it relates to World War II.

Following his graduation from high school in Sonoma Valley in 1973, Michael was a Communication Studies major at California Polytechnic State University in San Luis Obispo, California. Michael received recognition and won several awards for speech writing and delivery during that time, and chose to follow a career in journalism following college and his enlistment in the U.S. Navy.

Today, Michael is an author, screenwriter, and radio personality. He lives in Santa Rosa, California, with his wife, Angela, and son, Thomas.

Jean-Marie Heskett (Faggiano)

Jean-Marie and her family entered the gates of Santo Tomas Internment Camp in Manila, Philippines, on January 14, 1942, and were liberated on February 3, 1945.

Jean-Marie lives in retirement today, after working over thirty years as a quality inspector at Hewlett-Packard/Agilent Technologies in Sonoma County, California. Jean-Marie loves to travel and speak to groups about her experiences as a POW during World War II.

LaVergne, TN USA
04 February 2011
215377LV00003B/28/P